THE SCANDINAVIAN HOME

THE SCANDINAVIAN HOME

Interiors inspired by light

NIKI BRANTMARK

CICO BOOKS

LONDON NEW YORK

For Per

Published in 2017 by CICO Books
An imprint of Ryland Peters & Small Ltd
20–21 Jockey's Fields   341 E 116th St
London WC1R 4BW   New York, NY 10029

www.rylandpeters.com

10 9 8 7 6 5 4 3 2 1

Text © Niki Brantmark 2017
Design and photography © CICO Books 2017

A CIP catalog record for this book is available from the
Library of Congress and the British Library.

ISBN: 978-1-78249-411-9

Printed in China

Editor: Gillian Haslam
Designer: Louise Leffler
Photographer: James Gardiner

Senior editor: Carmel Edmonds
In-house design assistant: Kerry Lewis
Art director: Sally Powell
Production manager: Gordana Simakovic
Publishing manager: Penny Craig
Publisher: Cindy Richards

CONTENTS

INTRODUCTION

I first visited Scandinavia at the age of eight, when I went with my family to visit friends in Sweden for the summer. The long days were spent in an idyllic cluster of rustic red and white cottages by a lake in Dalarna, north of Stockholm. Time stood still and we ran wild between the thickets of trees in the forest, bathed, kayaked, danced around a maypole with flowers in our hair, and ate freshly baked waffles with lingonberries. It was all about going back to basics, surrounded by people we loved. It was magical.

Twenty years on I met my Swedish husband and moved to Malmö, Sweden, which has been my home for more than a decade. My love affair with Scandinavia lives on.

It didn't take me long to appreciate the ease with which the Scandinavians create beautiful homes, applying their innate sense of style. Scandinavian homes are renowned for their clean lines and muted colors; for being aesthetically pleasing yet at the same time highly functional.

This book explores ten city, country, and vacation homes, which encompass this wonderful sense of style. While all the homes have certain points in common, each has an individual story to tell.

Whether it's a house by the sea in southern Sweden, a Danish apartment in the heart of Copenhagen, or a country home on an island overlooking the Oslo Fjörd in Norway, they are all incredibly well insulated in order to stay warm during the long months when temperatures plummet below zero. Scandinavia's short winter days give rise to a yearning for natural light, which accounts for the preference for light wood floors and white walls and ceilings, which reflect light around the home. And when the sun dips beneath the horizon, these homes are lit with dimmed lights and the warm glow of flickering candles.

In keeping with the Scandinavian love of nature, interiors are often layered with natural materials such as wood, leather, sheepskin, linen, and wool, which break up the clean lines while adding texture and warmth. During vacations, Scandinavians take the opportunity to enjoy nature first hand in simple cottages and cabins by the sea or lake, or in the mountains. Rural retreats are typically stripped back to the bare essentials. Some even lack running water and electricity, while others are a little more modern. But the goal is always the same: to be somewhere with few distractions and to lead a simpler life, surrounded by the tranquillity of nature and the people you love, just as I experienced all those years ago.

"It's better to take time layering your home with items that tell a story and have a sense of purpose."

It's a mindful, uncluttered lifestyle, and one that aligns well with modern thinking about sustainability. In many homes—be they urban, country, or rural dwellings—you will find only a few beautifully crafted, high-quality iconic design pieces, antiques, and flea-market finds made from natural, sustainable resources. All are pieces that stand the test of time.

It's the combination of classics and individual pieces that makes the Scandinavian homes in this book so interesting and eclectic. In many cases, their creativity goes way beyond the choice or arrangement of furnishings. Some projects took incredible vision and foresight, not to mention determination—for example, the demolition of a derelict 1960s cottage to be replaced with a fabulous modern beach cabin, or the creation of a bespoke kitchen using wood reclaimed from a barn.

Many of these homes also feature unique, handmade items, from paintings and sculptures to pillows, rugs, furniture, and even lighting. There is an art to selecting and combining such individual pieces. Some focus on a coordinated color palette such as the "rustic, brownish tones" favored by artist Maria Øverbye in her Oslo apartment. Others apply logic to their scheme-setting, such as Karen Maj Kornum's careful arrangement of countries and eras in her Copenhagen apartment.

Creating a beautiful, original interior is of course a time-consuming process, but as Helsinki homeowner Marja Wickman points out, "It's better to take time layering your home with items that tell a story and have a sense of purpose."

Visiting and writing about these homes has taken me on an incredibly inspiring journey, leaving me full of new ideas for my own home. Perhaps my key take-away is that it's worthwhile making the effort of finding something old or secondhand and giving it a new lease of life —whether a flea-market find or an entire house in need of TLC. It's opened my eyes to the possibilities of what's already out there, showing me how things can be transformed with a little imagination.

I hope this book inspires you to create your own beautiful Scandinavian-style sanctuary and to furnish it with unique, carefully chosen items that tell your story.

chapter 1

URBAN LIVING

Many take great comfort from the sights and sounds of the big city. And yet, at the end of the day, when the bicycles are stowed and the stairs to the apartment climbed, an elegant yet relaxed personal sanctuary awaits. Think clean, pared-back spaces with carefully edited furnishings, including beautifully crafted, iconic design pieces, which deftly marry form and function, and treasured finds. The tones are soft and muted and the textures largely natural. Unobscured, triple-glazed windows flood the space with natural light by day while keeping the cold at bay, and flickering candles add a warm glow by night.

BOHEMIAN CHIC

*"My home changes all the time,"
Karen Maj says. But one thing
remains the same: "I can see
that my children are happy
here—they have what they
need and they feel at home."*

A treasure trove of antiques, secondhand finds, and Danish classics form the basis of a light-filled family home for Karen Maj Kornum and her four children in the heart of Copenhagen.

From the second you step inside Karen Maj's apartment, you sense it's a relaxed, happy place. Indeed, what matters most to Karen Maj is that her four children—Magnus (13), Billie (8), Talula (7), and Nimbus (4)—feel at home. "I wanted a space where the children could really live," explains Karen Maj, owner and art director of homeware store and interior design business Another Ballroom. "I love beautiful furniture but I'm not precious about it. It doesn't matter if something gets lost or broken."

Karen Maj bought the 6,300-square foot (178-square meter) apartment in 2004 due to its central Frederiksberg location. "We feel at home here, my family live close by, and when we open the windows we hear the life on the streets below," she enthuses. "If you take a bike ride, you always meet people you know."

OPPOSITE: **A table from Karen Maj's childhood home, a pair of original 1940s camping stools with leather seats, and a rattan chair provide a comfy place where friends and family can sit and chat to Karen Maj while she's cooking.**

OPPOSITE: The wall-mounted metal plate rack came from India over 20 years ago and is used to store dinnerware and bottles, as well as to display decorative items. "It's a little messy, but very convenient. Everything is to hand."

ABOVE LEFT: A cast-iron Japanese teapot is ready for action beneath a row of hand-painted Royal Copenhagen mugs and a vintage picture.

ABOVE RIGHT: Geraniums and a selection of chopping boards catch the light from the large kitchen window. A simple filament bulb serves as a task light in the evening.

LEFT: The lowest shelves of the plate rack serve as a handy place to store dinnerware and items in constant use, including pots, bowls, and jars collected over the years.

"I really like so many different styles and genres of art. I like to mix a lot."

Situated in a listed 1880s apartment block, Karen Maj's home has high ceilings and large windows, which flood the space with natural light. Laid out over one floor, the apartment is made up of a kitchen, two sitting rooms, a large dining area, bathroom, and three bedrooms. An old warehouse window allows light to flow from the sitting room through to the combined master bedroom and home office, where Karen Maj runs her business. "The desk was created by one of our Another Ballroom designers," she explains affectionately. "The light bounces off the gold, making it come alive."

OPPOSITE: A treasured photo of Karen Maj's oldest son holding her youngest son hangs in a creative way on the gallery wall. "I like to do small things like this."
ABOVE: A Danish PK22 chair by Poul Kjærholm, with a sheepskin throw, provides the perfect spot for a quiet read.
LEFT: A vintage toy elephant, which Karen Maj's father enjoyed playing with when he was a child, rests on a bookshelf.

The walls are painted white ("it's elegant and easy to work with") and autumnal accents, including yellow, burnt orange, and gold, add color to the rooms. The combination gives the entire space a coherent look. Bright bursts of color come from a vibrant blue, mid-century daybed and a purple coffee table, giving the space character and demonstrating Karen Maj's relaxed attitude to decorating. "I've always been interested in furniture and design and used to love decorating my room, even as a child," she recalls. "I don't have to put in any effort, it just happens."

However, there's one thing she's not relaxed about: "I would never bring anything artificial into my home. You'd never see neon in here," she grimaces. "As a child I was often dressed in wool, and this has followed me into adulthood—I have an aversion to anything synthetic." As a result, materials such as wood, leather, sheepskin, wool, and cotton dominate the space.

You get the sense that Karen Maj has carefully selected every item in the apartment, whether it's because of its history or simply because she loves it. "I really like so many different styles and genres of art. I like to mix a lot," she confirms.

"I would never place eight identical chairs around a table."

PREVIOUS PAGES: **Art is important to Karen Maj. A gallery wall is covered with flea-market finds, illustrations, limited edition lithographs, and work by up-and-coming Danish artist Mathias Malling Mortensen.**
OPPOSITE: **Series 7, Wishbone, and J39 "The People's Chair" are grouped around a large dining table built by Karen Maj's brother.**
RIGHT: **Stems of eucalyptus have been treated with beetroot to create an arrangement that will last a lifetime.**

ABOVE: A treasured wallscape from Bless in Berlin is glued to the sitting room wall, giving the illusion of another room beyond: "It's one of my favorite pieces. Sadly I won't be able to take it with me if I move." In front, a classic mid-century Børge Mogensen daybed in purple adds a splash of color to the space, and overlapping sheepskin throws create a snug feel.

OPPOSITE: A large section of the wall has been replaced with magnificent vintage warehouse windows to allow light to flow through from the sitting room to the master bedroom and home office. An iconic Safari Chair designed by Kaare Klint rests against the wall.

Karen Maj has furnished the entire space with a fascinating and eclectic blend of objects, including antiques, flea-market finds, Danish classics, items from her childhood home, handmade pieces, and—in a remarkable example of resourcefulness—other people's trash. "It's amazing what people throw out," she laughs. "It helps that here in Copenhagen, every second month people leave items on their doorstep to be taken away by a removal service. If you do the tour before the truck arrives, you can find all kinds of treasures."

Using individual pieces is also an easy, effective way to emphasize design: "You see the form, the texture, and the materials more clearly," explains Karen Maj. But there is a knack to combining different styles successfully. "I stick mainly to Danish design but do mix in items from other countries, such as Morocco. I never mix items from different countries from the same era, though."

Karen Maj is a keen art collector, the prominent piece being an eye-catching trompe l'oeil that covers the back wall of the sitting room. She bought it from a Berlin gallery: "I chose it as a work of art. I really love it—it's a treasured piece."

In the dining room, illustrations, work by up-and-coming Danish artists, and limited edition French lithographs hang beside photos of her children. Beneath is Karen Maj's book collection, a mix of classic and modern fiction with some spines showing and others facing inward. "When I've read a book, I turn it around," she explains.

And just as her bookshelf is updated almost daily, her home is, too. "My home changes all the time," she laughs. But one thing remains the same: "I can see that my children are happy here—they have what they need and they feel at home." And to Karen Maj, that means the world.

ABOVE: A classic 1960s teak daybed/sofa by Danish furniture designer Poul M. Volther, upholstered in brilliant blue, was chosen by Karen Maj "for its shape." A yellow and white quilt from America has been hung on the wall above it to add another touch of color and to break up the expanse of white. The items on the windowsill prove that one person's trash is another's treasure—Karen Maj found the industrial lamp and concrete sculpture on the streets of Copenhagen.
OPPOSITE: The master bedroom doubles up as Karen Maj's office, from where she runs her business, Another Ballroom. An elegant

Snoopy table lamp by Italian industrial designer Achille Castiglioni is used for task lighting at night. Natural light flows through the upcycled warehouse windows from the sitting room area and catches the metallic gold stripes on the bespoke desk made by an Another Ballroom designer. Karen Maj has artfully combined iconic Danish design pieces, including a Safari Chair and Wishbone Chair CH24, with a vintage Moroccan Beni Ourain rug and industrial bedside lamp. A Bobby Pillow from Lucky Boy Sunday, fluffy sheepskin throw, and a rattan lamp break up the clean lines and add a soft, natural touch to the space.

"*If you use individual pieces, you see the form, the texture, and the materials more clearly.*"

OPPOSITE: The charming light-filled children's room is enhanced by an oversized mirror made by Karen Maj's father, which hung in her bedroom when she was a teenager. Two painted wooden stools are also from her childhood home. Characterful pillows from Lucky Boy Sunday, a vintage Moroccan rug, and dressing-up clothes add texture and vibrancy to this wonderful room.

ABOVE LEFT: A child's crib and an armoire from Karen Maj's own childhood are now used by her children. A vintage plate rack has been cleverly transformed into a place to store children's books.
ABOVE RIGHT: An old pipe suspended from the ceiling with string provides a perfect place to store and display the children's colorful array of vintage dressing-up clothes.

DRAMATIC ELEGANCE

From the outside, the Notkin family's three-story architect-designed townhouse appears identical to all the others on the pretty tree-lined street in Frederiksberg, Copenhagen. Step inside, however, and you are immediately transported into a world where the rich elegance and glamour of 1920s Art Deco merge with classic mid-century Danish design to create an alluring space, which is as beautiful as it is practical.

Home to jewelry designer Rebekka Notkin, husband Christian Jensen, designer and owner of Monstrum, children Ella and Oskar, and dog Elton, this 1930s house in the heart of the Danish capital is a rare find. Laid out over four floors, it includes a basement and a ground floor with entrance hall, kitchen, and sitting room, which opens out onto a back garden—one of the features that first attracted the family to the property in 2014.

A magnificent black and white staircase leads to a small landing and three bedrooms. Almost going unnoticed is another door leading through to a surprising "home within a home," which includes Rebekka's study. "The silence and hidden space are perfect for creativity," muses Rebekka, who uses the light-filled room to sketch, cut paper, paint, and sew. Beyond this, and up a further narrow, little staircase, lies the magical master bedroom.

OPPOSITE: **A wall painted in "Grape" by Flügger and the Danish National Museum sets the scene for a cozy sitting room, made up of an Eilersen sofa upholstered in wool, a limited edition "The Spanish Chair" by Børge Mogensen, and a green marble coffee table by Danish designer Dennis Marquant from OX Design.**

RIGHT: "Within The Landscape" —a magnificent piece by Danish photographer Astrid Kruse Jensen—hangs above an elegant 1930s drinks cart "bought for its beauty." OPPOSITE: The balance between different textures plays an important role in this interior. A classic sofa by Arne Jacobsen, upholstered in a textile by Kvadrat, and chairs from Flötotto have been combined with a dining table by Danish architect Grete Jalk.

"I wanted to create a home with a special atmosphere, and dark colors are a perfect backdrop for the items my husband and I have collected over the last 20 years."

The Notkins moved in three years ago and have redecorated the house while being careful to preserve the original 1930s features, including Oregon pine wood flooring, sliding doors with brass details, and black marble windowsills. Despite this, they have achieved a unique style, driven by Rebekka's passion for the strong geometric shapes, bold colors, and lavish embellishment of 1920s Art Deco. Or, as Rebekka so eloquently puts it, "An époque where art and architecture gave weight to both elegance and functionality."

For Rebekka, it's "the luxurious and surprising diversity of this style and the many compositions of patterns, materials, and shapes" that are such a huge inspiration for her jewelry collections, personal style, and home. "I love the patterns, the

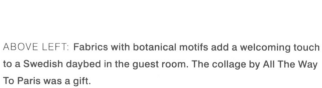

ABOVE LEFT: **Fabrics with botanical motifs add a welcoming touch to a Swedish daybed in the guest room. The collage by All The Way To Paris was a gift.**
ABOVE RIGHT: **"Mauritius," Rebekka's dream fabric by Pierre Frey.**
OPPOSITE: **A ceramic pot from a local flower market, bought for its color, delicate pattern, and size, provides the perfect home for a fig tree in the entrance hall, where an elegant staircase leads up to the next floor.**

colors, and all the details you find in art, interiors, fashion, and jewelry from that time," she explains.

The elegance and stylish avant-garde feel of the Art Deco era are particularly evident in the entrance hall, sitting room, and master bedroom, all decorated in the intense, rich colors that Rebekka describes as "bold and calm" in equal measure. The same dark brown floor features throughout the house.

Scandinavian homes are usually synonymous with white —and one could argue that the Notkins' home isn't typically Scandinavian if it were not for the beautiful, iconic Danish pieces seen throughout the house. "I wanted to create a home with a special atmosphere, and dark colors are a perfect backdrop for the items my husband and I have collected over the last 20 years," explains Rebekka. The dining room alone has been furnished entirely in mid-century Danish design classics, including a PH lamp, table by architect Grete Jalk, and Arne Jacobsen sofa (chosen for their "design, texture, quality, and beautiful details"), which pop against the

The master bedroom is decorated in the intense, rich colors that Rebekka describes as "bold and calm" in equal measure.

petrol blue wall. The dramatic tones also create a wonderful setting for the abundance of plants, art, vases, and treasured items.

Textures such as silk, velour, wool, wood, brass, and marble sit side by side throughout the room to create interest and a warm and inviting feel. "The soft surface on marble, the heavy weight in textiles, the combination of materials, and the balance between different textures play an important role in my interior," explains Rebekka.

Rebekka is also fascinated by pattern: "I really love patterns and color. The patterns in the work of Sonia Delaunay are my favorite inspiration. She is one of the most important female artists of the early twentieth century; she balanced art with fashion in such an avant-garde and stylish way," enthuses Rebekka, who likes to combine symmetrical and random patterns. In the guest bedroom, botanical themed cushions by Italian, British, and French designers are placed alongside a more formal pattern on a large screen—a picture of Rebekka's boutique in Bredgade, Copenhagen, where she produces and sells her jewelry. Botanical patterns can also be seen in the master bedroom, where they offer a stark contrast to the black furniture and vibrant

PREVIOUS PAGES: **Textiles bought in Milan add a cozy touch to a Wengler rattan chair and bed in the master bedroom, which occupies the top floor of the house.**
OPPOSITE: **Ella's bed came from her great-great-grandparents' house. Vintage prints from schoolbooks found in a bookstore many years ago have been framed and hung above the bed.**
ABOVE: **The peaceful home office provides a place to sketch, cut paper, paint, and sew. "The silence and hidden space are perfect for creativity."**
LEFT: **Some of the tools used in Rebekka's work as a goldsmith/jewelry designer.**

Cycling is a popular form of transport in Scandinavia, particularly in Copenhagen, which is recognized as the cycling capital of the world. The flat nature of the city and prolific cycle paths make it an easy way to go about your daily business come rain or shine (and, as I've discovered, in the snow, too!).

pink wall, while Rebekka's fabulous shoe collection and examples of her eponymous, custom-made jewelry add touches of glamour to the space.

On sunny days the family emerge from the enchanting, cool interior of the house into their green and tranquil garden, at the end of which a marble table and mid-century chairs provide a perfect haven for homework, morning tea breaks, and dinner with friends.

Frederiksberg's central location provides the family with the perfect base from which to explore the local park, the city, or simply go about their daily lives by bicycle. "I really enjoy being a family with kids in the middle of Copenhagen. Everything is nearby: sport, shopping, restaurants, green parks, and it's all in easy reach by bike," enthuses Rebekka. "I enjoy the feel and spirit of Copenhagen."

LEFT: **Built in 1934 by Danish architect Thorkild Henningsen, the building's listed façade bears details in the original "Frederiksberg Green."**
OPPOSITE: **Classic Danish garden chairs from the 1950s and a marble table from Italy provide an idyllic spot for dinner with friends in summertime.**

RELAXED
ARTISTIC

OPPOSITE: **Maria's apartment is furnished with a blend of iconic pieces, including the Tom Dixon Slab Chair, NAP Chair by Fritz Hansen, and DKR Wire Chair designed by Charles and Ray Eames, all of which are to be found in the dining room. A 11-foot (3.5-meter) long eighteenth-century wooden bench runs along the back wall, providing plenty of seating around a table, inherited from Jörgen's grandmother. A Flos 265 wall lamp and a painting by Maria draw the eye upward.**

There's something magical about artist Maria Øverbye's apartment in the old working neighborhood of Kjelsås, north Oslo. From the moment you step into the cocoon-like hallway, you're transported into a world full of secrets. The hallway is painted in matte black, enveloping you in a sense of mystery. "It has four doors so it always felt really cluttered," says Maria. "I painted it black to create an exciting, mystic feel. It all seemed to come together, and instead of seeing the clutter you see the black wall."

In striking contrast to the dark entrance, each door off the hallway opens up into a white, light-filled room. Immediately to the left, you find a bathroom and bedroom. To the right, there's a second bathroom and a kitchen, which has an open-plan dining area looking out over a roof terrace.

At the far end of the open-plan room there's a daybed and small office area, which can be cordoned off to create a separate guest bedroom. "I like to read books and magazines on the daybed," explains Maria. "I can also sit at the computer while my husband makes dinner, and we can chat." Double doors lead to a spacious sitting room and Maria's bedroom beyond. "I like to sit in my room and write in my diary, read magazines, and calm down. It's so nice to have a bedroom that's all yours, so you can be alone from the world when you need to be," she says.

Maria and her husband Jörgen, a teacher, have lived here since 2002. They have two daughters, who are both at college. Aurora, the youngest, visits at the weekends; Embla lives in the basement.

Large windows and vast ceilings reflect the building's heritage as a nineteenth-century school. This feeling of space is what first attracted Maria to the home. "Not many houses have 11-foot (3.5-meter) high ceilings. It really allows you to breathe," she muses. The tall windows reveal breathtaking views across Norway's capital city, including dense forest punctuated by the Holmenkollen ski jump in the distance. "They always built these old houses in good places. They were aware of locating them so they were a little raised, so you get fantastic views," explains Maria.

The apartment has a laid-back feel, enhanced by the time-worn white paint on the floor and doors where you can see a hint of the original woodwork. "The building is already full of history, but I like to add history from our lives here," Maria explains. "My children were able to play without worrying about damaging anything—and each nick and scratch bring back a memory." The bedroom walls have patches of rough plaster juxtaposed with smooth white paint. "I like my home to feel unfinished," she says. "I love the patina of soft gray plaster. It makes it a little rougher, which I think is beautiful."

The apartment is furnished entirely with secondhand finds, and no two pieces are alike. This is as quirky as it is charming. "I've never thought about it, but I never buy two of anything," Maria considers. "If you have one awkward piece it won't work, but lots of awkward pieces together create coherence."

"Like many Norwegians, I want my home to have a clean, minimalist look. Having many textures in the same room makes it welcoming and interesting."

LEFT: **Shelves by Swedish company String are laden with crockery and glassware collected from all over the world.**
OPPOSITE: **Maria has shunned standard kitchen units, preferring to use individual items found over the years. A little wooden table found at Oslo's Vestkanttorget flea market over 20 years ago sits beside a modern range oven. A vintage industrial task lamp helps to light up the area in the evening.**

"The building is already full of history, but I like to add history from our lives here. My children have always been able to play without worrying about damaging anything— and each nick, mark, and scratch bring back a memory."

ABOVE LEFT: An antique chest is used to store smaller items in the hallway, each drawer identified with chalk lettering. "We use it for everything. It's so nice to have."
ABOVE RIGHT: Maria loves lamps and her large collection can be seen throughout the apartment. A light, created by her daughter Aurora from iron waste, is used to illuminate the dark hallway.

The most prominent example of her eclectic approach is the lighting, which includes an array of mid-century, vintage, and antique fixtures. Maria has collected them from local flea markets as well as cities all over Europe and as far away as America. "I've been collecting lights since I was 25. I used to find them in local markets, but now I go to Belgium, Copenhagen, Amsterdam, Paris, and Vienna. I always come home with a new lamp," Maria laughs. "Every fixture brings back memories—and I talk about them in the same way some people talk about their tattoos."

You see the same laissez-faire attitude in Maria's use of texture. The sitting room alone features leather, sheepskin, wood, stone, clay, wool, linen, and other textiles. "Like many Norwegians, I want my home to have a clean, minimalist look. Having many textures in the same room makes it welcoming and interesting," she explains. This look lends itself to a coordinated color scheme, which Maria always considers when selecting pieces. "I'm conscious that it has to be rustic and brownish. There's a lot of wood, black, white, gray, and iron—that's why it comes together," she says.

ABOVE LEFT: Jörgen loves to sit and read with a cup of tea or a tot of whisky in a brown leather chair found at an Oslo flea market 18 years ago. The 1960s black wall lamp was found in an antique shop. Overhead, modern storage has been used to display a series of family photographs, drawings, and postcards.
ABOVE RIGHT: A clay, metal, and thread sculpture made by Maria is displayed in the dining area. "It's about shame, immobility, and also strength in life," she explains.

Because Maria is an artist, it's not surprising that artwork plays such a prominent role in the living space, adding to the apartment's unique and personal nature. Maria's oil paintings and clay sculptures (created in her atelier at the end of the garden) hang beside work by local Norwegian artists and photographers. "It's great to swap art. My paintings are expensive and theirs are too—so we just swap ones at the same price. That way they get things they want and I get things I want," she reasons.

Both Maria's daughters attend art college, and several of their pieces are on display. A portrait Aurora painted hangs in the guest bedroom. "She was only 17 when she did it, and it's lovely!" says Maria proudly. Maria believes her daughters' artistry comes from their creative upbringing. "I ensured they always had drawing paper and pens, and my atelier door was always open," she recalls. "They would sit and draw and paint next to me while

PREVIOUS PAGES: A table bought at Vestkanttorget flea market in Oslo lines the back wall of the sitting room and displays a wealth of treasures, including a ceramic egg sculpture by Maria's aunt, Ragnhild Winsvold, a 90° floor lamp by Danish brand Frama, and a Snoopy modern table lamp by Achille Castiglioni. A fascinating gallery wall made up of a horse picture by Maria's friend, photographer Anja Niemi, a poster of a man's foot being born by Robert Gober, and an oil painting by Maria adds drama to the area. A Willy Guhl Loop Chair can be seen to the left of the desk.
ABOVE LEFT: The "sister" sculpture by Maria occupies a chair of its own in the corner of the room.
ABOVE RIGHT: A bird skull from Rydeng Shop in Oslo, owned by one of Maria's friends.
OPPOSITE: Maria and her artist friends like to swap artwork. In the sitting room, a large abstract painting by Brita Skybak has been propped against the wall, and serves as a striking backdrop for a Danish chair by Hans Olsen from Modern Tribute in Oslo.

"*I like to read fiction or sit and stare into the fire as I knit sweaters.*"

I worked. I also made sure they always had something creative to do, such as dressing up, DIY, and crafts. They were never on a computer."

The family enjoyed many of these artistic activities in the large sitting room, which remains a favorite spot for creativity. "I like to sit and stare into the fire as I knit sweaters," Maria muses. "I also like to read fiction." Maria is an avid reader—although when it comes to stories, the apartment and its unique collection tell the best tales of all.

PREVIOUS PAGES: **The 11-foot (3.5-meter) high ceilings create a light and airy feel in the sitting room, formerly the headmaster's living quarters in the old school. A vintage industrial lamp bought on eBay is used to light up a photo by Benedikte Ugland of an old lady from Gudbrandsdalen, a traditional district in the Norwegian county of Oppland. A Børge Mogensen Hunting Chair offers a seat by the fire, which is kept alive from a stack of firewood accessed by a ladder.**
LEFT: **Antique industrial Jieldé lamps by Jean-Louis Domecq bought at a French market serve as reading lamps.**
OPPOSITE: **Maria's bedroom is a personal haven, and somewhere she can go to "be alone from the world." A dramatic photograph by Anja Niemi hangs over the bed. Stonewashed linen bedding in earth colors and a cardigan that shrank in the wash—"it's too small for me but it's so beautifully made it became a sculpture on the wall instead"— add warmth to the space.**

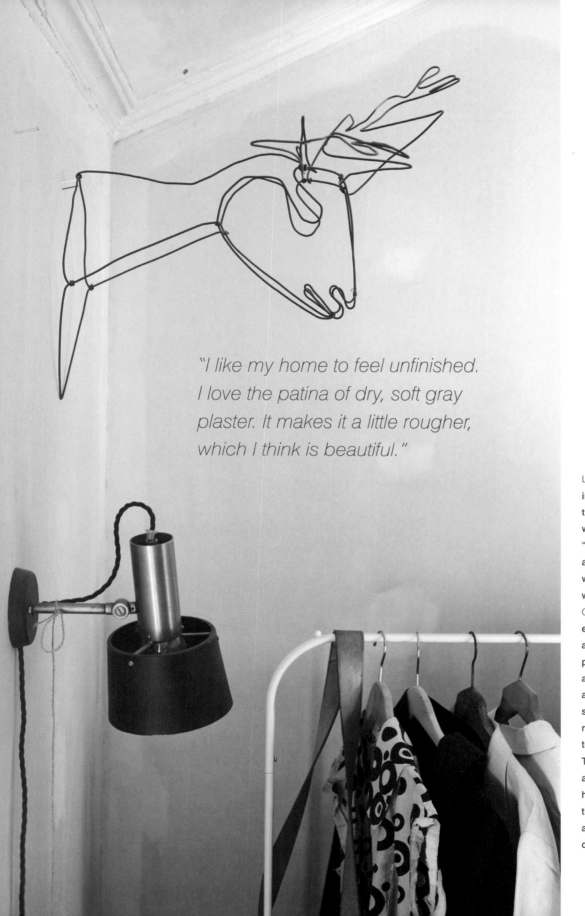

"*I like my home to feel unfinished. I love the patina of dry, soft gray plaster. It makes it a little rougher, which I think is beautiful.*"

LEFT: **A wire deer's head bought in Oslo and an antique lamp thought to be German juxtapose with a rough plastered wall. "I think it's so beautiful when an exclusive lamp contrasts with a rough wall—they work well together," says Maria.**
OPPOSITE: **A lovely area at the end of the open-plan kitchen and dining area is used as a place to relax during the day and can be partitioned off with a sliding door to become private sleeping quarters at night. The rust, ocher, brown, and gray tones are typical of Maria's style. Two oil paintings by Maria and another by her daughter, Aurora, hang on the gallery wall above the bed, and a chair found in an antiques store in Copenhagen doubles up as a bedside table.**

SLEEK
MINIMALIST

Marja and Marco dreamed of creating a unique, loft-style house designed to perfectly fit their lifestyle and needs. In the spring of 2013, their dream finally came true when they found a piece of land in a leafy housing area just outside Helsinki, Finland.

"The location was perfect. It was near the city, and the land was just the right size," recalls Marja, an art director and interior design blogger. Marja drew up the plans for a modern, two-story house, enlisting architect Tarja Petäjä to help achieve their dream build right down to the last square inch. In July 2014, full of anticipation, the couple moved in with their golden retrievers, Otto and Viljami.

The ground floor features a cavernous open-plan living area, which includes a sitting room, dining area, and kitchen, a place Marja describes as "the heart of the home." An opening in each corner of the room leads to further rooms, including a bathroom, utility room, and a snug TV room which in turn leads through to a guest bedroom.

The most striking feature here is the series of floor-to-ceiling, wall–to-wall windows at the front and back. These flood the space with natural light—a sought-after resource during Scandianvian winters when the sun barely reaches over the horizon. They also draw the nature indoors, creating a seamless feel between the garden and ground floor. The front half of the house is open so you experience the property's full height, giving a wonderful feeling of space.

OPPOSITE: **A light from The Beat Collection by Tom Dixon hangs from the open ceiling above the dining area, which features an "About a Table" by Hay and dining chairs and stools found at a flea market. Behind this, an opening leads through to the TV room.**

LEFT: **When Marja designed the house, she included a designated nook for firewood. The stacked wood is slightly raised off the floor to make it easy to keep the area clean. Textures play an important role in a minimalist space and here a slim Sinnerlig cork bench from IKEA provides contrast to the surrounding concrete.**
OPPOSITE: **Large floor-to-ceiling plants bring the nature indoors and break up the sleekness of the run of glossy white kitchen units.**

Contrary to popular belief, concrete is an eco-friendly material. It doesn't deplete natural resources, it's recyclable, it's poured locally, and it uses less energy than other floor types. It's also durable, easy to clean, and great for indoor air because it prevents mold and mildew. What's not to love?!

"You don't typically see concrete in a Finnish home. Finns prefer parquet or wooden floors," explains Marja. *"We chose it because we wanted to use raw materials."*

A magnificent polished concrete feature wall rises up through the center of the house, spanning the entire height of the property and obscuring the stairs to the upper floor. The nuances and textures in the rich, smooth surface dance in the light, making it come alive. Although frequently considered cold and industrial, in this home the use of concrete feels right, making a perfect partnership with the sleek surfaces, glass, and abundance of plants.

Set into the concrete wall in the open-plan area is the fireplace. As the days shorten and the weather gets colder, a roaring log fire creates a wonderful focal point in the room, and a cozy area for the couple to

"We have a lot of Finnish design in our home, such as brands like Iittala, Artek, Saana ja Olli, and 1kertaa2."

curl up and wile away the evening. A redundant space under the stairs and just to the side of the fireplace is used for a neat stack of chopped firewood, while the damper and soot hatch are hidden out of sight in the adjoining bedroom, ensuring an ultra-clean finish.

The statement wall is matched with a poured, polished concrete floor to complete this sleek and contemporary interior. "You don't typically see concrete in a Finnish home. Finns tend to prefer parquet or wooden floors," explains Marja. "However, we chose it because we wanted to use raw materials."

RIGHT: Glossy white Domus kitchen cabinets create plenty of storage space so that the white quartz countertop can be kept clear for a sleek look. A Flos Mod 265 wall lamp by designer Paolo Rizzatto can be angled to wherever directional light is needed. An antique wooden cupboard found at a secondhand store and a market bag add warmth to the otherwise monochrome open-plan living space. Displayed on top of the cabinet is a bold ABCD-B print by Playtype.

Marja and Marco are drawn to natural shades, choosing a strict gray-scale palette of "white and gray with a hint of black for contrast." Plants have been arranged in groups on the floor, ledges, and cabinets to bring nature inside and add a lush green accent to the monochrome space. "I think plants bring more life to the calm interior," explains Marja. The different-shaped leaves break up the formal lines of the architecture. Similarly, natural textures like cork, linen, wool, and wood add coziness and soften the concrete and white-washed walls.

Carefully edited furnishings and accessories ensure a highly functional yet minimalist living space, which, true to form for a Scandinavian home, is as practical as it is aesthetically pleasing. "We have a lot of Finnish design in our home, such as brands like Iittala, Artek, Saana ja Olli, and 1kertaa2," enthuses Marja. These design pieces sit alongside the odd vintage find, including an antique wooden cabinet discovered in a secondhand store. The result is a truly personal, pared-back look and feel.

In the kitchen, utensils, appliances, and crockery hide in ultra-sleek white units. "My husband and I love to cook but like to keep the work surface clean afterward. This is why we've designed our kitchen with lots of storage space," explains Marja. A large kitchen island adds to the storage while providing plenty of worktop space for prepping food, which is enjoyed at a round dining table, overlooking the terrace and garden.

PREVIOUS PAGES: **Natural light from either side of a vast concrete wall enhances the different colours and patterns on the surface. On cooler days a roaring fire provides warmth in the sitting room area—made cozy by a Hay Mags Sofa and Anno Jalpaikka rug designed by Susanna Vento.**

ABOVE: **Wall-mounted cabinets offer both sleek storage and a place for the TV, a Toad table lamp by Finnish brand Himmee, and a framed poster by Danish artist Silke Bonde.**
OPPOSITE: **A felt headboard from BoConcept, pillows by Saana ja Olli, and an AJ wall sconce by Louis Poulsen provide the perfect setting for bedtime reading. Beside the bed, an Iittala Plektra stool serves as a little bedside table.**

"I think plants bring more life to the calm interior."

Walk upstairs and you notice the light pine floor, which contrasts with the concrete beneath and creates an immediate sense of warmth. An open hallway lined with the couple's many books leads to the master bedroom. A centered wall separates the bed from a walk-in closet, where clothes neatly disappear behind doors. Beyond is a laundry room. "We can chuck dirty clothes into the laundry baskets out of sight, and clean clothes don't need to be carried to another space," explains Marja. Another example of the well-thought-out, practical nature of the house.

Back across the hall is a neat office used for blogging and as a creative space in the evenings. The desk is placed in front of the window, with views of the forest creating a calm ambience and the feeling that nature is never far away.

In June 2015 the pair added an outbuilding. Some would say it houses the most important element of a Finnish home: the sauna (reportedly there are more saunas than cars in Finland, with an average of one sauna per household).

LEFT: **Crafting tools are stored in a handy Uten Silo designed by Dorothee Becker in 1969.**
OPPOSITE: **The study, furnished with a Hay chair, cork storage boxes by Anno, and an M light found in a second-hand store, is where Marja oftens spends time during the evening and at weekends to blog.**

The façade of the sauna house is clad in stained black wood, which contrasts with the clean white finish of the main house, creating a sort of yin-yang effect. It appears both dramatic and cozy at the same time. Interestingly, neither Marja nor Marco uses the sauna regularly, preferring to sit outside on rattan chairs and soak up the morning sun. "We're pretty lazy when it comes to heating the sauna. We're not typical sauna users—we use it about twice a month, although perhaps more in the winter," says Marja.

Marja is a firm believer that a home is built over time, with items that have a sense of purpose rather than a "quick fix." She therefore sees her house as a work in progress and as a place that should be allowed to evolve organically. "Our home needs more layers, which will only come over time," she says. Thankfully, the pair "love to renovate and arrange furniture," although the house already feels very much like home.

LEFT: **Marja and Marco are keen gardeners. A modern hanging basket crammed with foliage hangs from a beam, bringing height to the outdoor space and decorating the path to the sauna house.**
OPPOSITE: **Rather than a luxury, saunas are seen as very much a part of daily life in Finland and as a place to relax with friends and family. Marja and Marco's sauna is housed in a modern wooden cabin with a striking black façade a few yards from the house.**

"The location was perfect. It was near the city, and the land was just the right size. Our home needs more layers, which will only come over time."

chapter 2

COUNTRY HOMES

With cities and towns just a cycle, drive, or even a boat ride away, it's the blue-gray sea stretching out as far as the eye can see or a deer foraging in the deep greens of the forest that inspire the country home. Earthy tones, wool, leather, wood, and linen materials soften the clean lines of the architecture. Floor-to-ceiling windows flood the spaces with natural light and draw nature indoors. Large, airy rooms are furnished with antique, flea-market, and inherited pieces, working together to enhance the history of the houses, each with a story to tell.

RENOVATED
SERENITY

"I love antiques and vintage items. I'd much rather buy a secondhand item with a story to tell than a new one that has come straight out of a factory."

As we arrive at Josephine Ekström's house on the west coast of Skåne in southern Sweden, the Öresund strait is awash with white horses and, in the distance, you can just make out the gray outline of Zealand in Denmark. The breaking waves create a wonderful, wild backdrop for this home and this setting is one of the reasons Josephine's house is so special. When we step inside, I'm immediately struck by the contrast between the interior and the surrounding nature. From the moment we enter the hallway, there's a feeling of absolute calm and serenity. "I like the way we live. It's close to the sea, and it gives me a feeling of fresh air and freedom," explains Josephine.

The white, two-story house was built in 1923. Josephine, an interior stylist and store owner, lives here with her engineer husband Rikard and their three children, Emmie (11), Noah (10), and Lily (6). When Josephine and Rikard bought the house eleven years ago, it needed total renovation. The couple painstakingly restored the house to its former glory, carrying out much of the work themselves, including completely re-tiling the roof. "Rikard's football team came to help us carry the new tiles up to the roof," Josephine remembers. They tore down two walls on the ground floor to create a bigger kitchen, and replaced the modern windows with originals from the 1920s. "We wanted the house to feel like ours," Josephine recalls.

The renovation also unveiled wonderful surprises. In the sitting room, when they stripped back the floorboards, they found the original black and red chequered tiles from the property's

OPPOSITE: **The original 1920s tiles were discovered under the laminate floor in the sitting room and relaid in the hall, where they serve as a reminder that this building was once the local general store. A leather chair by designer Kristian Vedel, bought at auction, and a German coat rack found at a flea market in Copenhagen are bathed in light from the windows.**

former life as the village general store. "We were so excited when we found the tiles under a laminate floor," explains Josephine. "My husband cleaned every single one of them. We were keen to use them somewhere in the house, so we re-laid them in the hallway."

The ground floor features a snug area, sitting room, bathroom, and open-plan kitchen and dining room, all of which lead through to each other in a circular layout. All the rooms have the same pine floor treated with a white, oil-based stain. At first sight, the walls also appear strictly white, but that first impression is misleading. When you take a closer look, you see subtleties and nuances in the deliberately uneven texture, creating a softness and bringing the walls to life. "I do like white. It creates a great backdrop for items with more color," Josephine explains, referring to the earthy, natural hues used throughout, such as pillows in ocher and olive green accents, which give the home a warm touch.

Color also appears in the unique pieces Josephine collects from auctions and flea markets. "I love antiques and vintage items," she enthuses. "I'd much rather buy a secondhand item with a story to tell than a new one straight out of a factory." You first see evidence of Josephine's keen eye in the hallway: a large gilt-framed mirror is propped casually against the wall opposite a sweeping staircase. "The mirror came from a castle in Denmark. I found it on a Danish auction site and was bidding against one other person. I couldn't believe it when the hammer went down at 1,200 DKK [US$180/ UK£145]," Josephine says gleefully. The German coat rack is another gem—the result of a morning's success at a Copenhagen flea market.

"I like textures. They make the whole interior look more interesting. My favorite materials are leather, linen, and velvet."

OPPOSITE: A voluminous Vapeur lamp makes a striking contrast with a Baroque gilt-framed mirror—originally from a Danish castle, it was acquired at auction by Josephine. Beyond, a mid-century Bertoia Side Chair designed by Harry Bertoia sits beside a door leading to "the snug," where a traditional Swedish tiled stove from Gabriel Keramik takes center stage.

RIGHT: Josephine's home is made up of individual pieces often found in flea markets or at auction. In the sitting room an eyecatching chrome Arco lamp designed by Achille and Pier Giacomo Castiglioni in 1962 extends over a Bold chair by Moustache and a vintage glass coffee table. A Moroccan Beni Ourain rug and Flexform Lifesteel sofa in brown leather add a cozy touch to the room. The mirror on the back wall was made by Josephine and Rikard (a similar one is available at Lily & Oscar).

These items set the tone for the rest of the house. The fascinating blend of iconic design pieces, mid-century finds, antiques, and handmade items creates a distinctive interior style. In fact, aside from the white walls, light wood flooring, and minimalist furnishings, it's not a typically Swedish interior. "We have a Swedish bed, and our kitchen cabinets are from IKEA, but I think those are the only items we have from my homeland," Josephine confirms. "Right now, I'm into Italian designers. They have a certain way of making furniture look elegant." This predilection for Italian pieces accounts for the Flos Arco lamp by Achille and Pier Giacomo Castiglioni and the Flexform sofa. "The sofa is one of my most expensive purchases ever, but I don't regret it for a second," she says.

You also see this eclectic, international style in the family dining area, where individual chairs—a mix of metal, fiberglass, and textiles—circle a marble dining table. The sitting room has a graphic look, with a Bold chair from Moustache and two large abstract paintings, which are Josephine's own work. "At the moment I'm into modern art. I like to create big paintings because they create a cool effect and break up the white walls," she explains. This room has soft tones thanks to the large vintage Beni Ourain rug from Morocco and the use of different textures

ABOVE LEFT: A pile of interior design books and magazines has been used as a plinth for an African tribal mask, discovered at a market in Paris.
ABOVE RIGHT: Light from the window highlights the contours of an Asian bowl, which has been filled with vintage French boules and two sculptures of hands, formerly used as molds for rubber gloves.
OPPOSITE: The owners have painstakingly restored the house back to its former glory, which included installing replicas of original electrical fittings. Paintings by Josephine, "inspired by a visit to Louisiana Museum of Modern Art in Denmark," break up the white wall and provide a dramatic backdrop for a pair of chairs with a footstool by Kristian Vedel, draped with a vintage zebra-skin throw.

like leather, velvet, clay, and marble. "I like textures. They make the whole interior look more interesting. My favorite materials are leather, linen, and velvet, among others," Josephine explains.

Throughout the house Josephine has artfully arranged sculptural objects, rounded ceramics, glass bell jars, and African masks in interesting vignettes on windowsills, countertops, and even on a pile of magazines. These catch the light, add warmth, and give the house a comfortable, personal feel. For example, a shell on the glass coffee table, also bought at auction, serves as a reminder of the coastal location and complements the harbor view.

Walk upstairs and you notice a softer, perhaps more feminine feel. There's an immediate sense of space. Here Josephine and Rikard knocked through several walls and raised the ceiling height to create a large, L-shaped, open-plan office and communal living area, where the family like to watch TV and hang out. The lovely exposed wood beams and pale gray floor add to the light and airy, yet cozy, ambience. The communal workspace near the stairs is bathed in natural light, offering the perfect spot for work and homework and for storing company papers.

As with the ground floor, there's a distinct ethnic touch to the upstairs rooms. This is most prominent in the large glazed clay pots and patterned pillows, which are arranged on a white linen sofa and on the bed in the master bedroom. "I like ethnic patterns like the old African embroidered designs on my cushions. They're all different and so beautiful," Josephine explains.

The master bedroom feels rather romantic. The bed is made with layers of stonewashed linen, each layer peeled back to reveal a different earthy hue. Matching linen curtains collect in a pool on the floor and are drawn to one side to show a view of the gray-blue sea.

PREVIOUS PAGES: **Family meals are enjoyed around a marble table which is pooled in light and surrounded by a mix of chairs, including a Dorsal Stack Chair by Giancarlo Piretti and Emilio Ambasz, a mid-century Eames Side Chair, and a Charles and Ray Eames Wire Chair. An iconic Verner Panton VP Globe pendant lights up the area after dark. Beside the table, a gallery wall adds interest and breaks up the white walls.**
ABOVE: **Vintage glass domes bought from an acquaintance who imports French antiques have been used to display paintbrushes and a paper giraffe.**
OPPOSITE: **In the upstairs sitting room a sofa from Svenssons i Lammhult has been draped with white linen—"We bought the sofa 20 years ago and it still works for cozy family evenings," says Josephine affectionately. A fluffy Beni Ourain rug adds softness underfoot, and is occasionally sprawled on by the kids when there's no space left on the sofa. A papier-mâché pot from China and patterned pillows from Africa add a distinct ethnic touch to the space. Large doors painted in matte black lead through to the master bedroom.**

"I like changing my style over the years. It stems from my childhood—I used to love re-arranging the furniture in my bedroom, and still do today."

Most of Josephine's work is centered in her studio and shop, which are in a converted garage and open to the public for several hours each week. A lush, landscaped garden surrounds the studio. "The family who built our house were keen gardeners—they created different zones and even dug a pond," she explains. "When we bought the house, we changed lots of the plants. I like hydrangeas, roses, and boxwood, so the flowerbeds are mostly made up of these." There's also a patio, which dates back to the early 1920s and provides a sheltered spot for meals during warmer months.

These original features form the backbone of the beautiful family home you see today. But the furniture and layout will only look like this for a fleeting period because Josephine loves to swap things around. "I like changing my style over the years. It stems from my childhood—I used to love re-arranging the furniture in my bedroom, and still do today," she says. In fact, its potential is one of the things Josephine appreciates most about her house. "I love that there are so many possibilities for changes inside. I'm planning to tear down a wall between our sitting room and kitchen. I just have to convince my husband first," she laughs. But Josephine doesn't make any change for the sake of it —every adjustment is aimed at helping the family feel relaxed and happy in the house. Because as Josephine says, "The most important thing is that we all love coming home."

PREVIOUS PAGES, LEFT: **A desk made up of a heavy emperador marble slab resting on wooden trestle table legs made by Rikard pops out against the light gray and white backdrop. An original fiberglass Eames Side Chair DSW provides the perfect spot for homework, paying bills, and other activities under the glow of a 1950s Mantis lamp by Bernard Schottlander. An urn, used as a plant pot, is one of many dotted around the house.**
PREVIOUS PAGES, RIGHT: **Layers of stonewashed linen in earthy colors contrast with pillows covered in striking African textiles. Next to the bed, a vintage brass lamp base partnered with a velvet lampshade by Christina Lundsteen sits atop**

a white Eero Saarinen bedside table. A beautiful antique statue, given to Josephine by a friend of her mother, adds a rather romantic feel to the space.
OPPOSITE: **Josephine is a big fan of linen. In the bedroom she has combined sheer linen curtains in cream with brown, white, and dusty pink bedding to soften the straight lines of the room. Wooden beams and a rustic stool add warmth, while a filament bulb sets off the simplicity of the space.**
ABOVE: **An open clothes rail is used to store and display some of the prettiest clothes, which have been hung on simple copper hangers in their eldest daughter's room.**

ELEGANT
GRAY
SCALE

Located on the beautiful Danish riviera, the Grut family home is inspired by magnificent views of the Öresund strait on one side and lush forests on the other. A soothing gray color scheme forms the backdrop for rich patterns and textures, iconic design pieces, modern items, and family heirlooms, creating an awe-inspiring home that is both calm and inviting.

You arrive by a road that snakes up the eastern coast of Zealand from Copenhagen. The buzzing city streets lined with rows of houses and apartment buildings slowly fall away to make room for hedgerows studded with wisteria, foxgloves, and hollyhocks and eventually morph into small fishing villages similar to the one that Cille, an interior stylist, Peter, a CEO, and their three children—Frederik, Agnes, and Martha—call home.

Built in 1875, the house was formerly a summer cottage enjoyed by Copenhagen city folk. In days gone by people flocked to the seaside in the summer, traveling by horse-drawn carriages to escape the smog. These days, bicycles are the preferred form of transport. "We enjoy the fact that Copenhagen is only 7½ miles (12 km) away, since it gives us the opportunity to bike to the city," explains Cille.

The couple first went to see the house in 2003, and they were immediately drawn to its incredible views over the Öresund strait, the body of water that separates Zealand from southern Sweden. They also fell in love with the magnificent west-facing courtyard behind the house, which looks out onto the Jægersborg deer park, a UNESCO World Heritage Site. With its ancient oak trees and large population of red and fallow deer, the park is truly a beautiful sight.

OPPOSITE: **Positioned between two pillars in a wonderfully grand bay window, a bespoke dining table, which can be extended to seat up to twenty people, is circled by a set of Modern Beetle chairs by GamFratesi for GUBI. Flowers from the garden and a pewter tray picked up at a flea market in Paris catch the light streaming through the bay window.**

Cille and her husband have spent years meticulously renovating their house, being careful to stay true to the original features and unique ambience. "When we renovated, we did it with full respect for the house's architecture and style. All the fabulous stucco ceilings are original, as are the wooden floors," notes Cille.

The house has been decorated throughout in soothing monochromatic tones, inspired by the calm gray-blue and white of the Öresund strait. "I always think it's best to choose colors from the environment in which you are located, reflecting the area you look out on and the special kind of light that comes through the windows— whether it's an urban, seaside, or forest setting," enthuses Cille. "Here it's the sea and the forest, so we've used green, gray-blue, and shades of white."

The ground floor is made up of a hallway, dining room, kitchen, study, and sitting room—all incredibly spacious, airy rooms, emphasized by the light pouring through the large windows and the magnificent high ceilings. Each room has been painted in a different nuance of gray-

OPPOSITE: **This classic Danish Frits Henningsen sofa has been covered with a vintage Indian throw and pillows from H&M Home. Art photography by a Danish artist hangs over the sofa, adding color to the space.**
ABOVE LEFT: **Mouth-blown and handpainted Ballroom lights in smoke, pink, and army green by Danish brand Design By Us hang from the magnificent stucco ceiling.**
ABOVE RIGHT: **The wooden bench is by Cille's favorite interior designer Ilse Crawford and was bought at an exhibition at the design showroom The Apartment in Copenhagen.**

"My style is classic and functional. I like to keep furniture inherited from my family and mix it with modern Danish furniture—that's what makes it personal."

PREVIOUS PAGES: **The kitchen was designed by Cille to ensure it had the right look, with ash countertops resting on custom-made cabinets. A pair of &Tradition Blown pendants hang from the ceiling, silhouetted against a wall painted in Farrow & Ball's "Strong White."**
BELOW LEFT: **Dappled quails' eggs create a pretty display in a pewter-colored bowl.**
BELOW CENTER: **A denim blue cushion with a flower motif was handmade using fabric from Tapet-Café.**
BELOW RIGHT: **A magnificent glass cabinet inherited from Cille's grandfather has been painted and filled with an array of carefully selected family treasures.**
OPPOSITE: **A pair of vintage PK22 lounge chairs and PK33 stools by Poul Kjærholm sit beside an IKEA sofa. The painting is by Danish artist Mogens Andersen.**

beige (or "greige") depending on which direction the room faces, how the light falls, and how the family intends to use the room. The paint is Gloss 2, an incredibly powdery paint with a matte finish. On the east side of the house, Cille's study and sitting room have been painted in darker shades, while the west-facing dining room and kitchen carry paler hues along the same color spectrum. With one room leading into the next in a circular fashion through large double doors, there is a general sense of fluidity, balance, and harmony, echoing the body of water beside the house.

This abbreviated color scheme and the carefully edited choice of furniture allow the beautiful architecture of the house and the crisp Scandinavian light to do the job of creating a striking, yet irresistible

sense of calm. This is evident in the large dining/drawing room where the furniture has been dramatically scaled back, with just a cabinet and sofa at one end and a side table and simple wooden bench at the other. The focal point of the room is the large, round dining table, which is bathed in "the most magnificent light" from the bay window. A set of modern Danish design Beetle chairs designed by GamFratesi for GUBI make this a comfortable spot for family meals and entertaining between two floor-to-ceiling pillars.

Cille describes the overall style of the house as "classic and functional." The kitchen is perhaps the most prominent example of this. Open shelves line the back wall, which has been painted in Farrow & Ball's "Strong White" (don't be deceived by the name—it's actually a very pale gray!). Bespoke base cabinets are painted several shades darker and have a traditional look and feel, right down to the brass knobs. A simple ash countertop adds natural warmth to the space while providing a practical place to prepare the fresh, locally sourced ingredients such as the garlic, lemon, and herbs Cille favors.

The rest of the house is similarly pared back, yet it still achieves a charmingly lived-in feel thanks to the thoughtful mixture of furniture, which includes inherited pieces (as an architect, Cille's father also had a keen interest in design), iconic design classics, and modern design items, as well as some pieces of furniture that

PREVIOUS PAGES: **A wall painted in "Ammonite" by Farrow & Ball provides a calm background for a space where the family likes to gather around a magnificent traditional Swedish masonry oven. The sitting room has been furnished with a mix of classic design pieces, including a PK33 Stool and a PK22 Lounge chair by Poul Kjærholm and an Eva chair by GUBI. Cille regularly updates the IKEA sofa with different covers for a constantly changing look. A separate alcove has been painted in "Mole's Breath" by Farrow & Ball, the darker shade carving out a distinct study area.**

ABOVE LEFT: **A beautifully simple pendant light allows the intricately detailed stucco ceiling in the sitting room to take center stage.**
OPPOSITE: **A vintage wooden desk by Børge Mogensen and a KEVI chair are flooded with light in Cille's spacious home office.**

LEFT: The master bedroom is decorated in calming shades of gray to reflect the sea view, partially obscured by the lined silk curtains.

OPPOSITE, LEFT: An old bookcase has been given a new lease of life as a bedside table, painted in the same tone as the wall and adding to the light and airy feel of the space.

OPPOSITE, RIGHT: Cille plays with the tones along a gray scale throughout the house. In the master bedroom soft linen pillows in gray and white rest against a headboard upholstered in dark gray fabric for a soothing and inviting look.

"I love the feel of good-quality textiles and am addicted to natural materials such as linen, wool, and silk."

came with the home. "I think this mixture gives the house personality," explains Cille.

A striking example of this is in the sitting room, which contains classic mid-century Danish designs such as the PK22 chair and a pair of PK33 stools by Danish designer Poul Kjærholm, which Cille received as a birthday present from Peter. A fully functioning Swedish masonry oven, which came with the house and must have originally been shipped over from Sweden, creates a warm atmosphere in winter. In the back corner, a fantastic glass-fronted cabinet, inherited from Cille's grandfather and painted by Cille, is brimming with treasures such as antique silverware, a bust, and glass bell jars.

Cille uses the monochrome scheme as a backdrop, and then plays with eye-catching patterns and accent colors, adding accessories such as pillows and throws. "My choice of patterns changes a lot, but I keep coming back to graphic designs," she explains. "Right now in the sitting room it's ikat and more wild patterns, such as Joseph Frank for Svensk Tenn." Accessories are also used to update the look according to the time of year and mood. "It depends on the season, but a few new cushions can actually change your interior in a second," says Cille.

At the far end of the room, an eye-catching gallery wall has been painted in Farrow & Ball's "Mole's Breath"—a color designed to resemble a mole's coat. The darker shade helps frame the pictures, but also defines the separate zone —an alcove used as a study from which Cille runs her interior styling business. "I love working from home, but am most often on the run!" she exclaims. As with all areas of the home, this one is functional and fluid, doubling up as a space for the children to do their homework as well as an area to sew or paint.

A sweeping white staircase leads up to a long corridor, a junction for the bedrooms and family bathroom. Just like the rest of the house, the master bedroom has been decorated in different nuances of neutral gray, creating a wonderfully calm feeling. Contrasting textures similar to these can be seen throughout the house, where Cille favors high-quality materials such as linen, wool, and silk to generate a warm, inviting feel.

Here a set of long voluminous, double silk curtains are the one factor that Cille describes as "not typically Scandinavian." Since Scandinavia is plunged into darkness for many months of the year, light is at a premium, explaining why many choose not to obscure the windows at all, but opt instead for simple shades. On a sunny day, Cille's silk curtains are drawn back and the French balcony doors thrown open to reveal an incredible sea view and welcome the fresh breeze. In the future, the pair plan to build a larger balcony, which will extend the bedroom outdoors.

A courtyard at the back of the house has been covered with a large awning made by a local sail-maker. The magnificent canopy keeps the area shaded from the sun and sheltered from

LEFT: **Hand-painted ceramics from Royal Copenhagen are used for afternoon tea.**
OPPOSITE: **A canopy made by a local sail-maker provides shelter for an outdoor dining space where the family love to gather, rain or shine. The marble tables are handmade. "I never have to maintain them, they are outside all year round." The seating was made by Peter.**

Since moving to Sweden I've been a big fan of the turf roof and was excited to see one in the courtyard. Up until the start of the twentieth century, this type of roof was extremely common across rural Scandinavia, owing to its efficient insulation qualities. A modern version has surfaced as an environmentally friendly and attractive alternative to contemporary materials and is widely used on new-build cabins in Norway. It's also becoming popular in new city developments, adding a welcome touch of green to urban landscapes.

the rain. It also creates a cozy "outdoor room" for alfresco family meals, among wisteria, pansies, and lavender—deliberately chosen to match the same blue-gray color scheme of the interior. The black and white façade of the house rises up above the courtyard and, at the far end, an original sod roof has been carefully maintained—a reminder of the traditional turf roofs so common across Scandinavia in the nineteenth century and earlier.

The Gruts' home is constantly evolving. "Our lives keep changing a little bit at a time, and I keep being inspired in new ways," explains Cille. One thing that remains the same, though, is the proximity to the Öresund strait, offering cool daily dips and fishing excursions in the summertime, and to the lush forests of the adjacent park. Both are a constant source of inspiration for Cille Grut and her forever-changing family country home.

ABOVE LEFT: **The paved courtyard was one of the factors that first drew Cille and Peter to the house. The pair have worked hard to maintain the turf roof, traditionally cultivated for its insulating properties, and enjoy growing fresh herbs to use in the kitchen.**
OPPOSITE: **The family enjoys swimming in the Öresund strait from May until September. The colors of the water and forest surrounding the house form the basis of Cille's color scheme.**

"I always think it's best to choose colors from the environment in which you are located, reflecting the area you look out on and the special kind of light that comes through the windows."

ECLECTIC ISLAND LIVING

When you step into Tone Kroken's beautiful home, you immediately appreciate her sharp eye for distinctive pieces and knack for harmonizing different styles.

Her home is certainly unique. Situated on an island just off the mainland in Norway's Oslo Fjord, it's accessed by bridge—or rope ferry if you're arriving between May and October. "You have to pull yourself over," Tone laughs. "Sometimes the ferry is on the other side, and you need to pull it back before you can cross. This affects your mind set because you can't be in a rush. It sets the slower tone for the island as a whole."

The island is home to around 30 families who live there all year round. The numbers increase during the summer months, when more people arrive to spend time in their holiday cottages. There are no cars on the island, so locals walk, cycle, hitch a lift from one of the two tractors, or use a kick sledge when snow arrives. "When I traverse the island, I take in the nature, the setting sun, the deer grazing in the meadows. There's always something new to look at," Tone remarks.

LEFT: **Tone immediately fell in love with the peaceful location of the house. She enlisted the help of the late architect Lars Østigaard to extend the existing timber cottage in order to create a larger, split-level house. Floor-to-ceiling windows flood the house with natural light and draw in the beautiful nature. On warmer days the doors onto the terrace are thrown open and meals are enjoyed alfresco.**

"I travel a lot and buy anything I think is beautiful. I like to discover unique pieces that no one else has."

Many of the island's residents are creatives who have shunned the 9-to-5 work day for a more flexible lifestyle. "We're surrounded by singers, artists, and musicians," Tone explains, and this relaxed ambience is what first attracted Tone and her children, Emma (20) and Emil (21), to the island in 2002.

Initially, the plot was occupied by a small wooden cottage and a tiny log cabin. There was no running water or indoor bathroom. "We immediately fell in love with the nature, the quiet, and the tranquil atmosphere. I knew this was the perfect place for the kids to grow up," Tone recalls. She enlisted the help of the late architect Lars Østigaard to extend the cottage. Lars understood her desire to modernize it while maintaining the closeness to nature, which was one of her favorite things about the property. "Lars was a friend and a fantastic architect. We instantly fell in love with his drawing—I think we only changed one window. It's very light, and I love the feeling that inside and outside are one and the same," she enthuses.

The main house is split over three levels, connected by a series of small stairs. The extension on the lower level comprises a lovely open-plan sitting room, dining room, and kitchen. It's easy to see why this cozy space is the heart of the home and the place where Tone and her children gather. "We like to be close and listen to music, cook, and talk—we don't watch much TV," she muses. The room leads through an entranceway to a second sitting room in the original cottage structure. There are also two bedrooms and a shower room.

The master bedroom—which doubles as Tone's office—sits above the open-plan living space. A simple linen sheet half obscures the bedroom from the landing and upstairs bathroom. "I don't like having many doors in my home," Tone explains. "When the kids were young, it was perfect because we were always close to one another and we still like to hang around together today. Plus, the home feels more friendly and welcoming."

OPPOSITE: **The hallway is furnished with sentimental items including a portrait by Tone's daughter, Emma, and a mirror from her brother:** "It was a wonderful present and I think of him every time I pass it," **Tone enthuses. A Panton Quick Ship chair adds a modern touch and is a surprising contrast with an ornate mirrored table.**

The house's fluid nature creates a relaxed vibe. It's designed so each room's purpose can change based on mood, time of day, and season. For example, there's a small sofa in the family bathroom. "When the kids were young, we'd be in here every afternoon. I'd read to the children while they were in the bathtub, or we'd draw. It's a fantastic, sociable room," Tone explains. In winter, when the light is poor, she often moves her workspace from her bedroom to the dining area.

Tone opted for a soft color palette in the main house, giving the space a sense of calm. The floors are white with a touch of gray, and most of the walls, floors, and ceilings are painted a fresh white. "This is typically Scandinavian," she says. "It's because we have such dark winters but still want a cozy, light interior." However, Tone has peppered the home with darker tones, too. You see this in the bathroom's deep gray accent wall, as well as in the rugs, pillows, and paintings. "I love washed-out, earthy hues," she says. "My favorite accent color is a dirty, dark blue."

The paintings are mostly portraits, some of which have been created by Gøril Fuhr, who also lives on the island. "I always seem to fall in love with female portraits. They're very powerful," Tone comments. One of her favorite pieces is by her daughter Emma. This takes pride of place in the hallway. "I've always encouraged my children to be creative," she explains. "When they were young, we made sure they had pens and paper everywhere we went."

OPPOSITE: **A large dining table with sculpted legs, a linen Gervasoni Ghost chair, and another Panton Quick Ship chair create an interesting mix of textures and shapes in the all-white dining area. Floor-to-ceiling shelves built by a local carpenter are crammed with treasures, including a series of porcelain vases from a Chinese flea market and a collection of coffee table books: "I love interior and photography books—many were presents from friends."**

ABOVE: **A ceramic acorn and precious Buddhist sculpture—both bought in a flea market in Beijing—catch the light on the windowsill in the hallway. "I like Buddhas, they are so peaceful," says Tone.**
OVERLEAF: **The sitting room, located in the original section of the house, is mainly used when guests come to stay. A rustic garden table, picked up for 50 NOK (US$6/UK£5), is paired with a comfortable sofa, C1 armchair designed by Verner Panton, and a large Chinese armoire used for storage. A magnificent painting by Norwegian artist Elisabeth Werp occupies the space on the back wall.**

The understated color palette is the perfect backdrop for the furniture and accessories Tone has gathered from her travels. "I travel a lot and buy anything I think is beautiful," she enthuses. "I like to discover unique pieces that no one else has." The travel is mostly to garner inspiration for her work as an interior stylist. "I never visit interiors stores when I travel. I'm mostly looking at architecture, people, and unusual color and pattern combinations," she explains. You see an example of this in the master bedroom, which Tone has decorated with an eclectic array of furniture, including an Indian cabinet, an antique Italian chair, and a Norwegian side table. All these pieces coalesce in a beautiful, creative way.

Similarly, the main sitting room features a white linen Italian sofa, two vintage Tulip chairs, and a worn rug from a trip to Istanbul. "I love old rugs—the structure, the look, the history. Rugs are very important because they ground the room and can be used to create zones," she says.

Tone loves to visit flea markets and often returns to places such as Marrakesh and Beijing just for their wonderful markets. "I think I've been to Marrakesh and Beijing more than 20 times," she says. This explains the abundance of clay vases and Buddhas arranged on shelves, window sills, and ledges around the house.

OPPOSITE: **A large antique fairytale-like rug bought in Istanbul separates the sitting room from the rest of the open-plan space to create a zone where the family like to relax and listen to music on Tulip chairs bought at auction and a Gervasoni sofa piled with pillows. "I particularly like the gold sequin cushion—it adds a touch of glam and makes an ordinary Monday shine!" says Tone. A Danish Hay tray table lies in the center, and portraits by Tone's neighbor, Norwegian artist Gøril Fuhr, keep watch over the area.**
ABOVE RIGHT: **The focal point of the living area is a magnificent French antique fireplace bought from a friend in Oslo. The mantelpiece has been designed to display a collection of items including an oval-shaped mirror, initially "too new" for Tone's taste: "I placed it in the garden for two years—that's why it's so beautiful," she explains. A Chinese porcelain Buddha, another flea-market find, sits beside antlers found on the island.**

OVERLEAF, LEFT: **An accent wall in rough, dark chalk paint provides a dramatic backdrop for a French iron bathtub, acquired from friends. Tone uses it everyday in the winter. "It looks the same as when I bought it—old, rustic, and destroyed," she says with affection. A primitive stool and bust bought from a Swedish collector add to the relaxed, rustic feel of the space, while coral found on a beach in Greece serves as a reminder of the coastal location.**
OVERLEAF, RIGHT: **Tone's bedroom is made up of an eclectic mix of items, including a glass cabinet from India, an Italian antique chair, and a French-style side table as well as smaller, decorative details, such as a porcelain vase bought at a flea market in China. A linen sheet is used to separate the room from the landing.**

"I find Buddhas so peaceful. I buy them from a huge flea market in Beijing," she explains. In her quest for one-off pieces, Tone also taps into her huge network of friends in and around Oslo, including buyers and store owners who trawl far-flung places like Bali and Africa. "I'm always asking them what they have. Often I'll take the leftover pieces no one else wants. I'll do anything to avoid buying something completely new," she says.

Tone has an aversion to new items, so much so that she actively ages her pieces. "I liked the shape of the mirror over the fireplace but not the new look. So I put it in the garden for two years—it was under the snow. That's why it's so beautiful," she laughs. You can clearly see Tone's desire to surround herself with beautiful items that tell stories. "I like things to have history," she

explains. "In the house, everything seems to come together in harmony because I love each piece." That harmony—and that love—pervade every inch of her home.

As part of the building work, several trees were felled to reveal a spectacular view over the Oslo Fjord. Tone wanted to make the most of the breathtaking vista so she built a gazebo at the foot of the garden. One side is completely open and the others are glazed, so you can enjoy the view from every direction while being sheltered from the wind. The gazebo is decorated almost entirely in white, contributing to the light and airy feel. It has plenty of seating as well as two beds that double as a sofa. "I can start using the gazebo as early as April. I use it for reading and parties. I love to sleep there in the summer."

OPPOSITE: Tone has built a modern-style gazebo at the foot of the garden to take advantage of the magnificent views over Norway's Oslo Fjord. Much of the building has been constructed from windows reclaimed from an old property in southern Norway. The space has been decorated in soft, neutral hues to give it a summery feel and the sofa and armchair have been accessorized with fluffy pillows and sheepskins for a relaxed, comfortable vibe. A small round table from Marrakesh complements a larger table—formerly a dining table but now with shortened legs.
LEFT: A beaded necklace in soft hues from Bali hangs from a hook in the gazebo.
OVERLEAF: In the summer, family life moves outdoors. Tone has created several zones so everyone can relax and enjoy the incredible, ever-changing scenery, regardless of the weather. On warmer days family and friends gather together in the outdoor seating area where a fire pit is brought to life after dark. The gazebo provides shelter from the wind and rain and means the alfresco lifestyle can be extended from April all the way to October.

"We immediately fell in love with the nature, the quiet, and the tranquil atmosphere. I knew it was the perfect place for the kids to grow up."

chapter 3

RURAL
RETREATS

At holidays and weekends the hustle and bustle of the city is exchanged for a quieter life at a retreat by the sea or lake or high up in the mountains. Dwellings are typically small and fuss-free, designed for leading a simple life surrounded by nature and the people you love. Whether in the form of a rustic cottage, furnished with inherited and handcrafted items and cozy sheepskins, or a sleek, modern cabin that combines clean lines and contemporary pieces, the emphasis remains the same: easing the stresses and strains of daily life and enjoying the great outdoors, even if only for a few days at a time.

RUSTIC SUMMER COTTAGE

If you know where to look along the shore of the Tammisaari archipelago, you'll discover three pretty cottages nestled in the forest. Their red ocher exteriors, traditional in Finland's south and west regions, stand out from the surrounding trees. This is the idyllic summer retreat for a Finnish family of four generations ranging from two to 92 years old.

The family acquired the former farm in 1967 as a retreat in which to escape the stresses and strains of daily urban life, and they still use it to this day at the weekends and for vacations, or anytime their schedule allows it. The idyllic, remote environment has uninterrupted views of the surrounding waterways and is a perfect location from which to savor the luxury of simplicity and enjoy activities like gardening, forest walks, foraging, fishing, boating, swimming, and—for the children—building makeshift outdoor dens.

As with most Scandinavian summer cottages, the great outdoors makes up the bulk of the family's living space. Hammocks, tree houses, and little pathways decorate the rocky landscape. On the day we were there, a moose appeared through the mist— apparently not an uncommon sight. The family also shares the land with deer, foxes, rabbits, and even a pack of wolves. "They're growing in numbers, but I think they're more afraid of us than we are of them."

When the family bought the land, there was a farmhouse dating back to 1867 and a second cottage built in 1954. They built a third cottage in 2008 to accommodate their growing numbers.

OPPOSITE: **The original farmhouse dates back to 1867 and is the oldest cottage on the estate. The pine façade has been painted in** *punamulta* **or "red earth," named after the dye used in the deep red waterproof paint traditionally used on cottages and barns in this part of Finland. The house looks out over the beautiful Tammisaari archipelago, a series of islands in the Baltic Sea.**

FAR LEFT: **Gymnastic rings bound with leather, enjoyed by several generations, hang from the rafters in the main room.**
LEFT: **The family has worked hard to maintain the heritage of the building. A selection of late-nineteenth-century tools used to build the original farmhouse are displayed on the wall in the entrance way.**
OPPOSITE: **A rocking chair sits beside a World War II chest crafted by Finnish designer and sculptor Tapio Wirkkala. The doorway to the farmhouse kitchen has been used as a delightful makeshift growth chart, documenting the increasing heights of each member of the four generations of family who frequent the cottages.**

Each cottage has been painted in the same "Falu red." Known in Finland as *punamulta*, Falu red is a dye used to make dark red paint and is typically used on wooden barns and cottages in the area to protect them from water. White window frames complete the unified appearance of the cluster.

Despite these changes, the family is keen to pay homage to the history of the farm. The very tools used to build it hang in the entranceway of the farmhouse, a butter churn has been used as a decorative piece in the main living area, and black-and-white photos in the master bedroom show the cottage and the surrounding area in its pre-World War II days.

Downstairs, the exposed wood ceiling and pine flooring set a scene of charming simplicity. The space is decorated in rich earthy colors, including gray-blue, brown, and black with an enchanting blend of Finnish antiques, handmade items, and vintage finds. The wood floor has been largely left exposed with the exception of two long rag rugs. Commonly seen in cottages,

"In colder weather we use the big fireplace in the main cottage. Of course, we also have a sauna, which we warm up every single day."

"It's a family cottage so we have big meals almost every day. We smoke our own fish and buy fresh ingredients from local farmers."

the traditional rag rug is handwoven on a loom using recycled scraps of fabric (typically yarn or strips of cloth from discarded clothing, bedding, and drapery). An eye-catching circular rug made by a family member has been placed in front of the fire and a fourth rug—a magnificent Finnish *Ryijy*—hangs on the wall as a decorative piece.

The result is a relaxed, open-plan living and dining room with a hint of old world charm and a snug, cozy feel. The living area has looked pretty much the same since it was first decorated in the late 1960s. The one exception is a new L-shaped sofa, where the extended family likes to gather on cooler evenings and rainy days.

Beautiful wooden stairs lead up to two bedrooms. These are decorated in a nautical theme that includes striped curtains, pelmets, and pillows, ropes, anchors, maps, a fishing rod, and antique fishing buoys. "We've all grown up with the sea. Enjoying the archipelago by boat is one of our favorite pastimes, and we wanted to pay tribute to it indoors, too." By the window, a pair of binoculars hangs on the wall, ready to be trained on a visiting bird of prey or a boat gliding up the sparkling waterway outside the window.

The farmhouse is a popular retreat, and upstairs storage has been ripped out on either side of the rooms to create bunks for extra guests. At lights out, people pull curtains across for added privacy. The same fabric has been used as a practical way to hide the open storage space used for additional bedding, blankets, and clothes.

PREVIOUS PAGES: **A set of dining chairs, designed by Finnish interior architect and furniture designer Ilmari Tapiovaara, has been arranged around an antique dining table. An original Semi pendant lamp by Danish architects Claus Bonderup and Torsten Thorup, with its sharp, clean lines and geometric shape, hangs over the table, adding a modern touch. A circular rug, made by a family member, brings a jolt of color to the space.**
OPPOSITE: **A family rocking chair dating back to the 1800s sits in front of a beautiful handwoven *Ryijy* rug. *Ryijy*, meaning "thick cloth," is a traditional Finnish rug, with a history dating back hundreds of years. The color and decorative nature of the design are a unique part of Finnish folk art, and the rugs look magnificent as wall hangings. In contrast, a vintage butter churn is a reminder that this house was once a working farm.**

"We've all grown up with the sea. Enjoying the archipelago by boat is one of our favorite pastimes, and we wanted to pay tribute to it indoors, too."

ABOVE LEFT: **A beautiful set of traditional "Kuksa" drinking cups, naturally crafted from birch burl by Sami people, the indigenous tribe inhabiting northern Scandinavia and the Kola Peninsula of Russia, was given to the family as a present. All-purpose Kuksa cups are hand-carved and used by reindeer herders, hunters, and others on the move in the great outdoors.**

ABOVE RIGHT: **Antique fishing buoys, once used in the surrounding waters, hang from a nail, giving a nautical touch to the bedroom.**
OPPOSITE: **Original black-and-white photographs show how the farmhouse and its surroundings looked in the pre-World War II era. The room has been softened with curtains, a pelmet, and pillows in matching nautical stripes, reflecting the coastal location of the house.**

Fifty yards away, along an undulating grass path dotted with granite rocks, is the second cottage. Marginally smaller than the farmhouse, the downstairs has a kitchen, sunroom, sitting room, and bedroom.

The sunroom is perhaps the most used room—it's bathed in warm light and looks out over the water, making it a perfect spot for a cup of coffee and a quiet read. It's decorated in a simple, calm palette of coastal blue, gray, and white, mirroring the colors of the Baltic Sea. It has been simply yet invitingly furnished with a dining table, folding chairs, and several comfortable wicker chairs. The cottage's kitchen is relaxed yet functional. Open shelves line the length of the room and are bursting with pretty crockery, glassware, vases, and candleholders, which match the blue and white coastal theme. A TV room is a cozy refuge on rainy days. Upstairs there are two bedrooms.

Although incredibly compact, the third two-story cottage offers everything a family could need, including a sitting room, small dining area, and kitchenette on the ground floor, and two bedrooms on the upper floor. It even has a balcony and a little terrace, which acts as a private outdoor area in which to relax and eat alfresco. Since the sauna and shower facilities in the second cottage are accessed through an external door, the occupants of this cottage can use the washing facilities without the need to disturb anyone.

PREVIOUS PAGES: **The master bedroom has a strong nautical theme, which includes ropes, an anchor, and a model sailing boat emphasizing the laid-back island lifestyle and strong maritime culture associated with the area. Former storage space, on each side of the room, has been used for bunk beds in order to accommodate the growing family and the many guests who come to stay.**

OPPOSITE: **A second cottage was built in 1954 to create a living space for an entire family and houses the all-important sauna, which is enjoyed daily. As with all properties on the estate, it's been painted in the traditional red dye and features white-framed windows.**

ABOVE RIGHT AND RIGHT: **The family often socialize until the early hours. Although it never really gets dark in summertime, oil lamps are used to light the grassy pathways between the cottages when the sun dips beneath the horizon.**

"Plenty of friends visit us in the summer, so there are always lots of people at the table, often until the early hours."

OPPOSITE: **Simple folding chairs made from wood add warmth to an otherwise blue and white room and create a perfect spot for small family meals looking out over the archipelago. A portrait of a family member as a child hangs on the wall behind.**
ABOVE LEFT: **Glass candleholders rest on a pretty tablecloth from Bungalow.**
ABOVE RIGHT: **Fresh flowers draw the outside in and add a splash of color, as well as giving a lovely scent to the room.**

All the cottages have basic facilities. There are two outdoor dry toilets—the most common form in Finnish summer cottages. "They're very practical and don't require much in the way of planning permission," explained one of the family. Fresh water is only available in the warmer months; in winter, the pipes freeze, so there is no running water.

The three buildings do have electrical heating (something not all Finnish cottages have), but the family also relies on roaring fires. "In colder weather we use the big fireplace in the main cottage. Of course, we also have a sauna, which we warm up every single day."

The cluster of three cottages means that at least three families can live happily side by side in self-contained dwellings while also enjoying some much needed privacy. And yet they are also together as one larger, extended family with the opportunity to socialize and gather whenever the mood takes them, the

OPPOSITE: **The wrap-around windows mean the sunroom of the second cottage gets remarkably warm during the day. A rattan chair bought at auction in the 1980s provides a perfect corner for a quiet read or to listen to the radio. The door leads to a large outdoors dining area where the extended family likes to convene on balmy evenings.**

RIGHT: **The galley kitchen of the second cottage is lined with open shelving for a relaxed "grab and go" vibe. A pretty assortment of glassware and ceramics, including cups and saucers designed by Carl-Harry Stålhane from Rörstrand, is displayed on the shelf.**

children charging in and out of one another's houses, baking with grandma and grandpa one day or climbing trees with their cousins the next.

The entire family loves to gather at a large, communal table. "It's a family cottage so we have big meals almost every day. We smoke our own fish and buy fresh ingredients from local farmers. Plenty of friends visit us in the summer, so there are always lots of people at the table, often until the early hours."

After an evening of laughter and conversation, family and guests return to their bunks. Glistening lanterns hang between the cottages to guide everyone home, but the midnight sun usually offers the best light of all.

RIGHT: A third cottage was built in 2008 to accommodate the expanding family. Although relatively small, the highly practical and functional living space includes a kitchenette, dining area, sitting room, two bedrooms, and even a balcony and terrace, making it the perfect self-contained "home from home" for a young family.

Finland boasts more than 100,000 lakes, and many Finns like to spend the summer months in the countryside enjoying the tranquillity of nature. Accommodation is often simple— a basic cabin or cluster of cottages. The stresses and strains of daily life melt away as people spend their time enjoying activities like berry picking and fishing while reconnecting with family and friends.

OPPOSITE: A waterway leads to hundreds of small islands dotted with charming fishing villages in the Tammisaari archipelago, southern Finland. The family love to navigate the archipelago by boat and often return with freshly caught fish, which is then smoked and served for supper.

OPPOSITE BELOW: Small boats, ready for the next family adventure, are moored at the end of the garden.

RIGHT: "Dry" loos are a common and practical choice for Finnish summer cottage owners. The sheer amount of administration involved in securing sewage works, plumbing, and drainage so near to the water is prohibitively expensive and time-consuming. This estate has two dry loos —one behind the original farmhouse, and the other a few yards from the 1950s cottage.

RIGHT BELOW: The estate is surrounded by beautiful, uninterrupted nature, making it a truly idyllic setting—a world away from the stresses and strains of everyday life in the city of Helsinki.

MAGICAL MOUNTAIN CABIN

"I love the sense of being close to nature, the view from the large windows, and the silence and feeling of peace I get when I arrive."

When Marianne and Jon first discovered this timber cabin in Sjusjøen, a Norwegian skiing destination a short drive across the mountains from Lillehammer, it was completely run down and off the grid. "All we could see was forest. There was no road and no running water. It was very basic," Marianne remembers. "For the first five years, we had to bring our own water and ski down to the cabin from the nearest road."

But the pair loved the rural location and were convinced that it could be transformed into the ideal retreat from their regular home just outside Oslo, for themselves, their children Jesper and Ylva, and dog Stella. "Both Jon and I grew up not so far from here, so we have a lot of childhood memories of this area. Another advantage is that it's not too far from Oslo."

The original part of the cabin has two small bedrooms and a charming living room with a dining area and snug TV corner arranged around a fireplace. "Even though it's draftier at this end of the house, the children love to hang out here and play board games, read, and watch movies," says Marianne. Even so, the cabin felt a bit too small. "We spent a lot of time thinking about how we could extend it without losing its soul," she recalls. "In the olden days, Norwegian cabins were humble abodes, built from leftover materials, so we wanted to honor this tradition."

Their extension project was inspired by "seter"—simple Norwegian mountain farms used for summer pastures. "We wanted to build something similar to a 'seter,' but with a modern twist."

OPPOSITE: **An armchair inherited from Marianne's grandfather and a chair found at a flea market are in the perfect position to "sit and enjoy the shifting light and follow the moon over the hills." The small mid-century table came with the cottage. Marianne acquired wood from the local Svenneby Sag sawmill to create several side tables, one of which can be glimpsed in the background.**

The family enlisted the architect Benedicte Sund-Mathisen of Suma Arkitektur, who happens to be Marianne's sister, to extend the cabin. Benedicte helped with the re-design and some of the lovely interior details, such as the frameless windows. In 2014, their extension was completed. Made from Norwegian pine, it has more than doubled the living area. A spacious hallway, a large open-plan sitting room, kitchen, and dining area, two bedrooms, a bathroom, a sauna, and a cloakroom have all been added.

Despite its rustic look and feel, the cabin has state-of-the-art appliances, including a fully functioning kitchen and automatic sensor lights in the bathrooms. The polished concrete floor has underfloor heating, which can be controlled remotely by cell phone, along with the lighting in the cabin. "Since the concrete floor can take several days to warm up, we usually switch the heating on from our home in Oslo. We also like to turn the lights on just before we arrive so the cabin is warm and inviting when we get here," explains Marianne.

As with the majority of Scandinavian homes, the space is highly practical. For example, there's a built-in bench near the entrance that's perfect for removing snow boots. Large, built-in drawers under the sofa and double beds provide plenty of storage. And the dining tables have been made with the same materials and measurements so they can be put together when the family is entertaining large parties.

The real showstopper, however, is the array of wall-to-wall windows in the open-plan living area. One window spans the entire width of the sitting room, offering panoramic views of the valley, which stretches as far as the eye can see. "It was my sister's idea, and we absolutely love it," says Marianne, "When they arrived with the window, the snow was so deep they couldn't get down the track. We had to enlist the help of a tractor to bring it down to the cabin and then lift it manually into place!" she recalls.

Beneath the window, a sofa built by a local carpenter runs the width of the room. "I love to sit there, gazing at the constantly changing scenery. Occasionally I might spot a moose sauntering past."

Three more floor-to-ceiling windows in the living area offer magical views from all angles. There's also abundant light throughout the day, and the room's color changes according to the time of day, the season, and the prevailing weather conditions. "At Christmas, the snow reflects a bluer light because there's not much sun. In the fall, the cabin appears more golden yellow. It's both beautiful and endlessly fascinating," says Marianne.

OPPOSITE: The custom-made kitchen island, cabinetry, and shelves are constructed from reclaimed barn wood bought from a farm further north. Open shelving creates a decorative contrast to the concrete wall without obscuring it completely. A vintage industrial Signal Wall light and Zig-Zag floor lamp by Jielde from Fransk Bazar supplement the two ceiling filament light bulbs after dark.

The cabin's kitchen is also striking. It was made using wood salvaged from a local barn that the farmer tore down. "It took me ages to find the exact pieces of wood I was looking for. I wanted a gray, rough finish to give this rustic look," explains Marianne.

The family used the same wood in other parts of the interior, including the beds and sofa. In the kitchen, it was combined with a brass backsplash and concrete worktop. The result is a rich, pastoral feel with a nod to the old-fashioned style of a traditional Norwegian cabin. The tones are organic. Marianne describes the muted creams, grays, and browns as "natural, harmonious, calm, and raw." This neutral, understated palette allows the scenery to take center stage, drawing it inside so it feels like part of the interior.

Marianne describes the cabin's style as "humble, stripped-down, thoughtful, and slow." Natural textures are mixed throughout. Wool, wood, linen, silk, stone, brass, sheepskin, and concrete are all prominent. "I love mixing textures to create variety. For instance, smooth, hard concrete against rustic, old wood," Marianne explains. "It makes for interesting contrasts." Hand-crafted items sit alongside flea-market finds and inherited pieces, including Tolix dining chairs, Eames chairs, and a mid-century armchair. "I love the combination of old and new, and the way they're blended together," says Marianne.

Many of the materials come from the surroundings, fashioned by Marianne into decorative objects. "I find a lot of inspiration from nature and often try to recreate patterns and textures when I make things," she says. There is evidence of her creativity throughout the cabin, in everything from pillows and lamps to tablecloths, wall hangings, and tables. "I'm passionate about making things. Both because I like to explore materials and because the room has a special energy when it's filled with personal objects that tell stories," she enthuses.

OPPOSITE: The kitchen is made up of a blend of textures, including rough reclaimed wood and a bespoke concrete worktop made by Tunge Ting. "I like concrete because it's natural, easy to clean, nice to touch, and sustainable," says Marianne. A brass backsplash made by a local blacksmith has been treated with acid for an aged look.
ABOVE: Leather handles made from a vintage children's sledge harness complement the natural materials used throughout the kitchen.
OVERLEAF: The focal point of the sitting room is a panoramic vista over the mountainous Norwegian cross-country ski area of Sjusjøen. The family loves to sit and enjoy the view from a wall-to-wall window seat, made from reclaimed barn wood by a local carpenter. The seating area has been laden with pillows and sheepskins for a warm and cozy feel. The bench also doubles up as storage.

"I'm passionate about making things, both because I like to explore materials and because the room has a special energy when it's filled with personal objects that tell stories."

Marianne's way of life is reminiscent of what many now call "slow living"—a sustainable, mindful way of being. This is central to Marianne's business, Slow Design, and it's also the family's philosophy when they're staying in the cabin. Marianne explains, "I see slow living as a mind-set; it's driven by an ambition to take the well-being of nature and all living creatures into consideration when making decisions. It's about enjoying the true beauty around you and finding that beauty in the little things. This approach helps me see what I have to hand, and how I can reuse it. To be creative, using your own hands and skills to make the things you need is also a part of it. It not only gives great pleasure but also makes me aware of the real value of things," explains Marianne.

There are signs of slow living all over the cabin. In the sitting room, balls of yarn lie waiting and ready, and it's heart-warming to see Marianne's daughter, Ylva, following in her mother's creative footsteps. "She's started with hairbands," says Marianne.

OPPOSITE: **The family enjoys meals at the ash dining table with steel legs welded by a local blacksmith. Sheepskin throws add a soft, comfortable touch to galvanized Tolix chairs which were bought cheaply and unused from a hotel. The overhead Z1 pendant light by Ay Illuminate creates interesting patterns and soft lighting after the sunsets.**
ABOVE LEFT: **A tray of "sustainable, organic, and recycled yarn" is kept to hand in the sitting room for whenever Marianne feels inspired to make something.**
ABOVE CENTER: **Marianne uses yarn from an "old Norwegian spæl" (Old Norwegian Short Tail Land)—a breed of sheep dating back to the Viking era—to create lampshades with beautiful textures and varied nuances, which illuminate the cabin with a warm glow.**
ABOVE RIGHT: **Many of the pillows on the window seat have been knitted, woven, or sewn by Marianne from leftover material, wool yarn, vintage military blankets, and linen.**

LEFT: The children prefer hanging out in the original section of the cabin. Pillows made from sacks by textile artist Heidi Bjørnsdotter Thorvik line an L-shaped bench, and sheepskin throws have been draped over three Eames DSW chairs. A lampshade made from loosely felted raw wool by Marianne emits a soft light in the evening.
OPPOSITE: Part of the old timber exterior can be seen in the hallway and is now used to store coats and outdoor gear. A stool from Marianne's childhood home has been draped with reindeer skin. "It's common to take reindeer fur on excursions to use as a seat pad, as it's lightweight, warm, and takes up little space in a backpack." Vintage ski poles come in handy when the snow is particularly deep, and a macramé wall hanging made by Marianne adds a decorative touch.

"Even though it's draftier at this end of the house, the children love to hang out here and play board games, read, and watch movies."

Despite the rural location, the family is never short of things to do. When Marianne and Ylva aren't busy with handicrafts, they spend as much time outdoors as possible. "In the summer and fall, we go hiking and sometimes hunting. Or we pick blueberries, lingonberries, and cloudberries. We eat around the campfire, relax, and live closer to nature," Marianne enthuses. "There is always work to be done at the cabin, whether it's stacking firewood for the winter or doing repairs. And the children are busy building tree houses and planning adventures, like sleeping outside."

In the winter, the valley is blanketed with snow and the family loves to go cross-country skiing. "It's one of the best areas in Norway for cross-country skiing since there's guaranteed snow all winter. When we return home, we usually have a sauna to warm ourselves up," says Marianne.

Ultimately, being at the cabin is about savoring life's simple pleasures. "For me, the biggest pleasure of all is fetching my dog Stella and my wooden skis and going off the beaten track." As the famous Norwegian saying goes, "We do not go 'out', but 'in' to nature." And it's a saying this magical cabin embodies.

LEFT: The furnishings in the bedroom have been kept simple, and the windows curtain-free: "We have no neighbors on this side of the cabin. It's wonderful to wake up surrounded by nature in the morning," Marianne enthuses. The bed has been made with natural linen and ex-Norwegian Army blankets. One of Marianne's knitted lamps, connected to a thick ball of yarn on the floor, lights up the bedroom after dark.

Marianne's way of life is reminiscent of what many now call "slow living"— a sustainable, mindful way of being.

OPPOSITE: The modern extension, was inspired by the humble Norwegian "seter"—a simple mountain farm building found high up in the summer pastures. Large modern windows reveal the wonderful nature, and a sliding barn door shields the indoor dining area from sun. On warmer days the family enjoys lunch at a simple pine table and bench set on the terrace.

ABOVE LEFT: The family loves outdoor life at the cabin. A primitive chair on the porch has been draped with reindeer fur for a cozy place to sit and enjoy the view the whole year round.

ABOVE RIGHT: A pair of wooden cross-country skis are propped up against the wall of the original timber cottage, which is more than fifty years old. The structure was moved from its original location in Fornebu, near, Oslo to Sjusjøen in the 1960s.

MODERN BEACH HOUSE

Perched high up on a cliff on North Zealand's beautiful, rugged coast, Naja Munthe's cabin is the perfect antidote to her hectic life in Copenhagen, Denmark, where she lives and runs her fashion design business, Munthe. Several hundred feet below, the gray-blue Kattegatt Sea stretches as far as the eye can see. "My life in the city is very hectic—kids, school, work, inspiration, shops, trucks. When I come to the cabin, I can completely forget about everything," Naja smiles.

Naja, her boyfriend, and the four children they have between them often visit the cabin for a day at the weekend and during vacations. "I chose this location for its wild, unspoilt nature and its proximity to the city—just a 45-minute drive. Plus, it's very laid-back, and there are lots of children here," she enthuses.

When Naja first bought the land in 2005, it was occupied by a small dilapidated summerhouse, which she tore down. She enlisted the help of famous Danish architect

LEFT: **Naja tore down the original cottage and, with the help of Danish architect C.F. Møller, built a modern beach cabin. Wall-to-wall glass offers magnificent views over the Kattegatt Sea. On warmer days the doors slide open to create a seamless link between inside and out, and the landscaped garden becomes an essential part of the living space. At night, the garden comes alive in the warm glow of firelight.**

ABOVE: **Primitive Argentinian chairs upholstered in cowhide make a striking contrast with the tiled floor and clean lines of the cabin.**
OPPOSITE: **The heart of the home is a cavernous living area made up of an open-plan kitchen, dining area, and a cozy sitting room, with a striking dark gray accent wall carving this out as a separate zone. Many of the items in Naja's home have been bought abroad, including a dining table from Italy and a wooden wall-mounted sculpture from India.**

C.F. Møller to help create her dream cabin. "I didn't want a traditional summerhouse with small windows. Instead, I wanted something more modern and out of the ordinary," she explains.

As with all Scandinavian vacation cottages, the great outdoors is an essential part of the living space. "I wanted to create the feeling that inside and outside were one and the same," Naja recalls. It was therefore important to create a picturesque garden, which they could easily hang out in. Naja worked with landscape gardener Designhave to create a series of zones, including a fire pit, dining area, and small seating area by the cliff, which is ideal for morning coffee. "They came up with the idea of small walls made out of plants. When you stand up you feel the wind in your hair, but when you sit down it's totally calm."

You enter the cabin at the back and step into a short hallway. Off the hallway there is a bathroom and a stairway that leads to an upper floor with two bedrooms.

At the end of the hallway, there's a long room with an open-plan kitchen, dining area, and living room. Three

bedrooms lead off the main room, one of which is an en-suite master bedroom. "I really like the layout and irregular shape of the walls. There are so many fun angles," Naja says of the design.

Wall-to-wall sliding doors with glass panels span the front of the cabin, and the family can pull them back to welcome the fresh sea air into the open-plan room. There's also an outdoor shower off the en-suite. "Before I built the summerhouse, I didn't shower outdoors. But I imagined it would be the most wonderful thing, and it has turned out to be," Naja enthuses.

A chimney containing an indoor and outdoor fireplace runs up the center of the house, and two gas fires can also be turned on to add light and a warm feel to the garden. "I love fires. Even if I'm here by myself, I light them and have a cocktail, glass of wine, or cup of tea. Then I sit for hours and do nothing except take in the sights, sounds, and changing weather," Naja muses.

"I don't think things have to come from the same place. A mask from Africa, chairs from Argentina—for me, the interesting thing is the merging of different directions."

OPPOSITE: **Black kitchen cabinets from Schmidt Kitchen make a striking contrast with the white countertops and walls. Two black GE Pendant Lights by Kartell help to light up the area at night. A painting by Elsa Sidsner has been placed high up on the wall to maximize height and draw the eye upward.**

ABOVE: Naja's success as a fashion designer is due to her creativity and incredible attention to detail, which filters down to her home where even the door handles are decorative. An example of this can be seen in the fridge door handle, which Naja created from a Syrian faucet. The rustic vibe is emphasized by the display of quirky objects —a cow's head looks over the kitchen from a vantage point above, together with a row of three masks found in Paris.

Throughout, the décor shows Naja's keen attention to detail. Even the door handles are special, fashioned from pieces she brought back from trips to India and Syria. "I'm an incredibly detailed person—you have to be to succeed in my industry. I think about details all the time, like how a button is sewn into a dress. At home, this becomes, 'How do I want to open the fridge door? What lighting do I need?'" she explains.

The lighting is the perfect combination of task, mood, and overhead. Dimmer switches make it easy to achieve the exact level of light required for a task. "I like lighting a lot—it can be used to create different moods and put a focus on areas like the dining table and kitchen," Naja says.

The detail makes the home truly personal, as does the eclectic mix of items picked up on Naja's travels to places like Thailand, India, Italy, Morocco, and Ibiza. "As a Dane, I'm inspired by Scandinavia. But I'm also inspired by my trips abroad. I bring a lot of stuff back," she laughs. "I don't think things have to come from the same place. A mask from Africa, chairs from Argentina—for me, the interesting thing is the merging of different directions."

Despite the exotic influences, the home has an unmistakable Danish identity, from the black wood façade panels to the clean architectural lines and pared-back look and feel. However, in recent years colors have started creeping in. In the sitting room,

OPPOSITE: **Old sofas upholstered in emerald green velvet add a subtle color to the otherwise monochrome living space, while a single cushion made by Naja adds pattern. Naja's home is teeming with exotic touches, including a decorative pendant light, an ethnic stool, and a beautiful photographic print of a lioness by Morten Koldby.**
ABOVE RIGHT: **A series of carved wood figurines from Africa make an interesting display in the bedroom.**
RIGHT: **A magnificent crystal on a light gray marble plinth on the coffee table catches the light.**

The Danish word *hygge*—pronounced hoogah—has cultural importance. It's used to describe the feeling of coziness and contentment you get when you surround yourself with the good things in life, such as family, friends, laughter, food, drink, warmth, and natural light. Naja's summer cottage is designed for hygge—the fire's warm glow, the soft lighting, the sound system. It really is somewhere you can switch off and enjoy the good things in life—alone or with the people you love.

there are splashes of emerald green. The master bedroom has dusty pinks and amber. "I've begun to incorporate more colors to add a warm feel to the living space," Naja explains.

As with many minimalist spaces, textures also play a vital role in adding warmth. In Naja's cabin, materials such as concrete, cowhide, wood, and linen sit side by side, adding interest. "You can tell I'm a designer. I care a lot about patterns and textures—it's in my DNA. When I create clothes, it's about touch. As soon as you take something in your hands, the feeling, texture, and fabric become important. In my home, I like to play with different surfaces to create something unexpected. I like an element of surprise, using combinations you don't expect to see in a cottage."

LEFT: **A sliding door is pulled back to create the feeling of sleeping under the open sky. On cooler days, Naja can lie and watch the changing shape of the sea through the glass façade.**
OPPOSITE: **An ocher throw from Swedish brand Himla and light pink linen pillow covers bring subtle accent tones to the master bedroom. A pair of decorative mosaic marquetry bedside tables from Morocco, inlaid with exotic wood and mother of pearl, have been placed beneath a pair of brass pendant lights from Senza, adding an ethnic touch to the space.**

Some of the textures help draw the surrounding nature indoors. For example, pebbles sit in a neat row on the kitchen window sill, half obscuring the wooden stairway leading down to the beach. "We always go to the beach because it's so amazing," Naja says. "Even in fall and winter, we wrap up and go for a long walk. The children sometimes protest, but as soon as we get there we all get lost in time. We can easily spend hours throwing stones into the water, climbing rocks, and building sandcastles."

And I get the impression she's not just talking about the beach. In a world where it gets harder and harder to switch off, Naja has created an oasis where she can lose sense of time. "It's like my pulse slows down. I can feel the kids are relaxed. It allows you to breathe more deeply. There's not much to do except enjoy nature."

And that is the very essence of the Scandinavian summerhouse.

"I like to play with different surfaces to create something unexpected. I like an element of surprise, using combinations you don't expect to see in a cottage."

OPPOSITE: **A custom-made bathtub next to a large window creates the feeling of bathing under the open sky. Above, a white sculpture bought in a Copenhagen antiques store breaks up the white wall. A simple ladder made from bamboo, used to store towels, and a rug from House Doctor add texture and a soft feel to the space.**
ABOVE: **An ornamental silver tray designed by Naja is used to display items such as beaded soap and candles.**

LEFT: From April to October Naja loves to take outdoor showers in the privacy of an adjoining outdoor bathroom. An antique millstone found at auction has been placed on the ground for a tactile feel underfoot. In winter, they turn off the water supply to prevent freezing pipes and use one of the two indoor showers.

OPPOSITE, LEFT: A primitive stool serves as a surface for a loofah, soap, and towel. A copper wall catches the light, its shiny surface juxtaposing with the stained black wood façade.

OPPOSITE, RIGHT: The cabin sits high up on a cliff overlooking the Kattegatt Sea, which stretches out as far as the eye can see. Stone breakwaters protect the beach at the bottom of the cliff, paving the way for long walks and family days out.

"I shower outside up until November. It's the most fantastic feeling when the warm water covers your body and you can see the rain and wind around you."

INDEX

Page numbers in **BOLD** refer to illustrations

PICTURE CREDITS

BOHEMIAN CHIC
Karen Maj Kornum, founder and owner
of Another Ballroom
www.anotherballroom.com
Instagram: @anotherballroom

DRAMATIC ELEGANCE
Rebekka Notkin, jewelry designer
Rebekka Notkin Jewellery
Bredgade 25
1260 Copenhagen K
Denmark
www.rebekkanotkin.com

RELAXED ARTISTIC
Maria Øverbye's home in Oslo, Norway
www.avsporing.no
maria@avsporing.no
Instagram: @mariaavsporing

Modern Tribute: www.moderntribute.com
Brokante: www.brokante.no; Instagram:
@butikkbrocante
Anja Niemi: www.anjaniemiphotography.com

SLEEK MINIMALIST
Marja Wickman
www.mustaovi.blogspot.fi

Architect: Tarja Petäjä
Designer: Marja Wickman

RENOVATED SERENITY
Josephine Ekström, interior stylist,
owner of interior shop Lily & Oscar
Lily & Oscar
Lerbergsvägen 37
Höganäs, Sweden
www.lilyoscar.com
support@lilyoscar.com

ELEGANT GRAY SCALE
Cille Grut, interior stylist
Instagram: @cillegrut

ECLECTIC ISLAND LIVING
Tone Kroken, stylist/interior decorator
www.tonekroken.no
Instagram: @tonekrok

Painter: Gøril Fuhr

MAGICAL MOUNTAIN CABIN
The cabin of Marianne and Jon Vigtel Hølland
Interior design by Slow Design Studio
www.slowdesign.no
Instagram: @slow_design

Architect: Benedicte Sund-Mathisen,
Suma Arkitektur

MODERN BEACH HOUSE
Naja Munthe, fashion designer
and founder of Munthe
www.munthe.com
Instagram: @muntheofficial

ACKNOWLEDGMENTS

It really does take a village. Firstly, I'd like to say a huge thank you to James Gardiner, for his absolutely beautiful photography. And to Julie Stewart for keeping up our spirits at 1.00am, lost on a Norwegian mountain road!

To the tremendous team at CICO Books, including Cindy, Carmel, Sally, Kerry, Gillian, and Louise, who have supported and believed in my ideas every step of the way.

This book would also not have been possible without the incredibly inspiring homeowners who graciously invited us into their homes and made us feel so welcome.

I'd like to thank my family, especially my husband Per, without whom I'd have never moved to Sweden and who endures my many interior ideas: "It's lucky our house is attached to the neighbors' or you would have torn it down and built a new one by now." My wonderful girls Olivia and

Alice and stepson Albin, who make our house our home.

My mother, who sat burning the midnight oil, reading through my texts (and Joanna le Pluart and Anna Gunning who also kindly looked over parts) and my father for looking after the girls so I could write, as well as my sisters Charlie and Cas.

I partly owe my passion for Scandinavian design to the Häggström family who welcomed me to Sweden all those years ago and gave me my first wonderful zest for Swedish life, and continue to be great friends today. And to everyone else who has made me feel so welcome in Scandinavia over the years, including my family-in-law and friends, of whom there are too many to mention by name.

And last but absolutely no means least, to everyone who follows my blog without whom this book would never have been made. This is my gift to you.